60 DAYS OF FRESH MANNA DEVOTIONAL

MARSHA MANSOUR

Editors: Stephanie Barrientos, Rose Ann Fusillo, Alexis Iglesias, Reina Clark, Susan Felegy, Druanne Glascott

Illustrator: Julio Barrientos

Formatter: Mavis Okpako

Table of Contents

Introduction

I'm so grateful to the Lord that you picked up this devotional! I want you to know that you've been prayed for and that we (the team) are believing God to meet you as you read the pages of this devotional. I deliberately didn't put any months or days in it, just numbers so that at any time you feel like picking it up you could just start knowing it is a fresh word for you every time! That's the heart of God, that every day he would give you a fresh word from heaven and that you would learn to depend on him one day at a time! So as you read this, let God meet you, let Him speak to you, let Him encourage you, and let Him move you to the next level! No matter where you are in your walk, my prayer is that you will go to the next level with God, step-by-step and day by day! May you know Jesus in the power of his resurrection! May you live the life He's called you to live! Know that Jesus loves you deeply and so do we!

His servant,

Pastor Marsha Mansour
Founder of Marsha Mansour Ministries

Fresh Manna for Each Day

Today, I want to tell you a story and you must listen to it with a different ear. It is a very common story that most believers will know. In fact, it is the title of this devotional. The title actually came from a friend of mine who listens to my vlogs. She said that the word that came was like manna, something fresh from God every day. Hearing that blessed me so much!

Let's start by understanding the concept of manna. Scripture tells us that everything in the Old Testament is for our learning. All of it is for us to deepen our understanding of the things of God. The story of the manna is very simple, but life-giving if we take a closer look. Israel came out of exile from Egypt and they were on their way to the Promised Land. Along the way, they complained about how hungry they were; they wanted to be filled. God said to them, "Do not worry. Every day, I will rain down manna and it will be enough for that day."

Manna was bread from heaven. The most delicious form of bread. It was full of nutrients and everything they needed to sustain them. Every day, they would go out and the ground would be covered with this manna. God gave them very specific instructions. They were to go out and take whatever they needed for their whole family. As much as they needed for all their meals, and for everything that they could eat THAT DAY. But, they couldn't take more than that. They could only take what they needed for that day. If they took more, it would rot. Oftentimes, they would try and hide some away because they were not sure that tomorrow's manna would come. When they did, they would wake to find it rotten and filled with maggots because they were not supposed to store it. They were supposed to trust that God would give them fresh manna every day. God did this for Israel for 40 years! For 40 years, every day when they went outside, there was fresh manna.

I remember praying over this story and asking God for a deeper word. God said to me clearly, "Know that manna is like My grace. Every morning when you get up, there is enough grace for whatever you will face. Whatever comes your way, I have given you the grace for it."

Do you know the origin of fear, anxiety, worry, and discouragement? They all stem from trying to live in tomorrow with today's grace. We do not have the grace for tomorrow, today. We get concerned about things that are coming in a month even though we do not yet have the grace for them. Every day when we wake up, we have manna for that day. We have the grace for that day. Through this story, God is saying to us, "Trust Me day by day, step by step. I will not give you the next 5, 6, 20 steps but I will take you one step at a time. Trust and be faith-filled. Know that, when tomorrow comes, I will give you the next piece and the next day, the next piece, and so on. Do not rush ahead or lag behind. Walk in sync with Me. Every day, I will give the grace you need to walk through what comes. Just trust Me."

The same way that Israel never went hungry or lacked food is the same way, child of God, you will never lack His provision. You will never lack having His manna for your soul. Whatever you face, child of God, you will have grace for it for the day. If you look too far ahead, it will overwhelm you and make you anxious. Why? Because you do not yet have the grace for it. When you wake up in the morning, you will have the grace for that day. So hold onto the Lord. Hold to this truth. Know that He will provide fresh manna for your soul every day. He will make sure of it because He is a faithful God, and you can trust Him every day.

Lets Pray: Father, I pray that You would encourage Your children and give them great understanding. Lord God, remove all anxiety, fear, and discouragement. Help them to understand that You have given them grace for the day in the same way You gave manna from heaven to Your people for 40 years in the wilderness. You will feed us every day by Your grace, by Your provision, and by Your mercy. Everything we need for what we will face in the days ahead, You have provided it. Father, we're not going to try and live tomorrow with today's grace. We recognize that if we do, it will not last, it will rot away. We pray, Lord God, for the understanding and ability to walk daily with You one step at a time. We bless You, Jesus. Amen.

God can help us any time in any situation

No Grasshoppers Allowed!

"We felt like grasshoppers in front of the giants, and so we became grasshoppers."
Numbers 13:33 AMP

Greetings child of God! I want to encourage you today by reading Numbers 13:33. Before we look at the verse, I want to give you some background on the story. Israel actually entered the Promised Land twice. The first time was when they left Egypt and reached it in eleven days. Upon arrival, they sent twelve spies to spy out the land, to ensure that it was indeed a good place, and bring back a report to Moses.

When they returned, they gave a good report. The land was everything that God said it would be. However, ten of the spies who went had an issue. They reported that there were giants in the land, and that they were huge! God did not tell them about these giants and they believed that they could not overcome them. However, Joshua and Caleb, two of the spies, agreed that the giants were there, but they also believed they could overtake them! These two felt that the giants were insignificant.

Joshua and Caleb, along with the ten other spies, gave their reports to the people. As one might expect, the voice of ten overpowered that of the two. Joshua and Caleb tried to convince the people that God was faithful, that He was bigger, and as a result, they would be able to rid the land of the giants. Consequently, because of the report of the ten, the people were unable to receive the good report of the two faithful spies.

Numbers 13:33 says, "We felt like grasshoppers in front of the giants, and so we became grasshoppers."

Hear that again, "We felt like grasshoppers in front of the giants, and so we became grasshoppers."

Isn't that incredible? They felt like grasshoppers. They felt small in the midst of the giants, and as a result, they became small. You know, that verse easily could have said, "We felt like lions in front of them and so we became lions." But it didn't, they felt like grasshoppers and they became grasshoppers. They forfeited the Promised Land and wandered forty years to find another way to enter.

Ultimately, all those people died and never entered the land of promise, except for two. The two who felt like lions: Joshua and Caleb. Forty years later, when the people of Israel came around once more to the promised land, a question was brought before Caleb.

"Is your sword ready to fight?" The people of Israel still had to fight the giants even though they wandered for forty years. The people asked, "Caleb, are you ready to fight?"

He said, "My sword has been drawn for forty years. I have been ready to fight those giants for forty years."

Child of God, I want to tell you something. In your walk with God, your victory and the things that you're going to walk after are going to come down to two perceptions: the size of your enemy and the size of your God. If you perceive the size of your enemy to be huge and overpowering, you will become a grasshopper every time. You will shrink back and become a grasshopper. But if you perceive your God to be bigger than any giant, you will be a lion.

Your perception is the difference in your walk, the difference in your warfare and the difference in your faith. You must choose the proper perception. If it is off, you won't walk in victory. On the other hand, if your perception is accurate and you declare, "I have an enemy, he's real, but God is bigger, greater and stronger. There is nothing too difficult for my God."

If you walk in that truth, you will be a lion. If your perception of your enemies are that they are huge, bigger and stronger, then you will be a grasshopper.

Let me tell you this, your enemy may be bigger than you, but he's not bigger than your God! Your enemy is not stronger than your God. Today, your God is able to do exceedingly, abundantly more than you can hope or imagine. Child of God, you don't fight for victory, you fight from victory. It is really important that you get the right perception and say, "Giants will come against me, weapons will be formed against me, but none will prosper!" There are giants that are going to come your way, but you are not a grasshopper, you're a lion! Understand today how big your God is, trust Him, and walk in victory. Your enemy may be bigger than you, but he's not bigger than your God. Don't be a grasshopper. Choose to be a lion!

Lets Pray: Father, I pray for everyone who is reading this today. I declare victory over their lives, victory over their circumstances Lord God, and I pray that whatever they're walking through, that they will have the right perception because this will dictate their speech, their prayer and their actions. I pray that You would anoint them, walk with them and lead them. Father, may they know how great and glorious You are, and that there is nothing You cannot do. May they trust You Lord. As they look at their giants, may they not feel like grasshoppers, but like lions instead. May they roar at what is in front of them because they know that You are for them. I declare victory over them. Father, I pray a special prayer for those that are struggling with sickness in their body. I pray healing over their body right now. I command their body to come in line with Your word, that from the top of their head to the soles of their feet, they are made whole, Lord God. Anoint them, touch them, fill them. I pray, in Jesus' name. Amen.

Fear the Lord

"The fear of the Lord is a fountain of life, turning a person from the snare of death."
Proverbs 14:27 NKJV

As I prayed for you and asked the Lord for a fresh word, I sensed Him prompting me to challenge your heart to be more like Jesus. I pray every day that the words on these pages will continue to provide nourishment to your spirit and you will grow and mature in the Lord.

The verse I want to share with you comes from Proverbs 14:27. It says, "The fear of the Lord is a fountain of life, turning a person from the snare of death." This verse is incredibly powerful! Maybe as you read the word 'fear,' you asked, "Does God actually want me to be afraid of Him?" It is not about us trembling before an oppressive and harsh God. That is not the picture we have here. You see, when we are in love with Jesus, so in love, the thought of displeasing Him breaks our hearts. This love will cause us to live in fear of not pleasing Him. We would say, "Lord, I want to be like you and I don't want to do anything that would offend you."

At times, we get things a bit backwards; we are so afraid about what others think. For a Christian, however, the fear of man is the kiss of death. We get into trouble if we spend all our time worrying about what people think. Our main focus should be on God, and what He thinks. Charles Spurgeon had a wonderful saying, "What has cured me of the fear of man is the fear of God."

So, how does this work?

If we fear God and live our life under the umbrella of His word, His truth, His character, and who He is making us to be, then the fear of man has no place. The fear of man, child of God, is something we cannot afford. If you have time to worry about what people think, it is evident that you are not spending time focusing on what God thinks. When we change our focus and ask, "God, what pleases you?" this change in focus will affect our attitude, our heart, our speech, and our thoughts.

If we spend time learning how to obey God and fear displeasing Him, then we will gain strength every day. This fear will literally save us from death. The snare of death will be removed from our life because we will not fall into traps set by the enemy to destroy us.

I live in the understanding of the fear of God. It causes me to bring my whole being, my thoughts, my speech, my heart, my attitude, and the way I treat others into submission to Him and Him alone. I am not worried about what people think. Instead, I am concerned about what God thinks. I do not worry about who will judge me, or how I line up with their values. I have made myself accountable to God and what He values. Before I speak, I must ask "Lord, is this going to please you?" Before I act, "Lord, is this going to please you?"

We literally live by the 'what would Jesus do' model of living. This is really what the verse means. The fear of the Lord is a fountain of life. Every time I operate out of the understanding of, "God, I want my life to please you, I want to look like you, I want to sound like you, I want to act like you," His life wells up within me, and death is removed from me. But every time I worry about what people think, or if I operate in my own flesh, then death works in me. On the other hand, if I take my thoughts, my heart, and my mind and submit them to the Father, then His life grows in me.

I live with the understanding of knowing that God will not harm me. I do, however, tremble because I love Him so much and never want to displease Him. This understanding allows me to operate from a place that produces life. My words and my attitude become life-giving.

The same thing will happen to you. As you become a fountain of life, your circumstances will be infused with the life that comes from Him. Your family will begin to live and your job will seem new. Everything around you will be affected. Conversely, if you live in the fear of man, death will creep into your situations and relationships.

If you live in this verse, "The fear of the Lord is a fountain of life and it will spare you from the snare of the fowler, the snare of death, will be removed," the result will be life changing. As you're walking, as you're living, as you're operating, start asking him, "God, how do I please you?" Because I want to tell you something, you can say you love Jesus, but true fruit of the love of Jesus is your obedience to Him. The fruit of love is obedience. So, as you operate in this fear of the Lord, you will begin to watch life spring forth into everything around you.

I challenge you, brothers and sisters, to live in the fear of the Lord and allow it to produce a fountain of life in you.

Lets Pray: Father, I pray in the name of Jesus that we would live in fear of displeasing you. I pray that our love for you grows so deep that it becomes our nature to simply obey you and not waste time concerning ourselves with pleasing man. Lord, let there be life, flowing in and through us, and to those around us. Amen.

The Currency of Heaven

"But without faith it is impossible to please Him,
for he who comes to God must believe that He is,
and that He is a rewarder of those
who diligently seek Him.
Hebrews 11:6 NKJV

Here on planet earth, the currency we use is money. We work all day to earn money. Why? So we can buy things: cars, houses, food, and anything we may need or want. This is how things operate here. Nothing moves without money.

There is also a currency in heaven – and it's not money. The currency of heaven is faith. Hebrews 11:6 tells us that without faith, it is impossible to please God. For anyone who comes to Him must believe that He is a rewarder of those who diligently seek Him. You see, faith is the currency that moves things in heaven. What faith says is I believe God is exactly who He says He is!

The Bible says that faith is the assurance of things hoped for and the certainty of things not seen. So, for God, faith is everything! When His children operate in faith, that allows God full access into their lives. Faith is the language God speaks. When He sees His children speaking that language, it allows Him to create freely in their lives.

He is a rewarder of those that diligently seek Him. People that diligently seek God are people that operate in faith. They have to believe in a God they cannot see. They have to live and pray to a God they cannot tangibly touch. Therefore, faith becomes an incredible seed in the life of a believer. It is how I get up every morning as well as how I live out my day. It becomes how I stand and pray. Faith becomes how I do everything!

That is our currency, child of God! If you want to be able to pray, stand, and live the life God has, you must learn to operate with the supernatural currency of FAITH. We are people of faith and we don't belong to this natural world. We serve a supernatural God that gives us access to supernatural things. We are people of the spirit and the way to move things in the spirit is by faith! If your heart is to please the Lord today, understand that we cannot please him without operating in faith! Become a powerhouse of faith!

Lets Pray: Father, help us today to be a people of faith. Cause us to increase in faith daily and to understand that faith is the language You speak. Help us to take big, faithful steps into all that You have for us! We love you, Jesus! Amen.

It's All About the Attitude

"Then my soul will rejoice in the Lord
and delight in his salvation."
Psalm 35:9 NIV

Blessings to you all! The verse I want to share with you today is found in Psalm 35:9. The verse says, "My soul will rejoice in the Lord, My soul will rejoice in the God of my salvation." I love this verse because I love the word will. The meaning of this verse is that it is a choice to be joyful. It is a choice to rejoice. There are times we think that our joy, happiness, gladness or the approach to how we will handle every day has everything to do with what's coming at us. There are many times in life when there is nothing to be joyful about. There may be a lot of things going wrong, but there is always something to be joyful about because Jesus never leaves His throne.

In many situations, it is your choice, child of God, to choose how you are going to respond. Your attitude is all about you. Your approach to things is all about you. You cannot control the things that come at you, but you can choose how you respond to them. Oftentimes, we choose to let those situations change us. We choose things that rob our joy and peace and it affects our ability to see our hardships as a temporary circumstance.

I am going to challenge you as a believer to live in the long game. You cannot live in the short game because, in the short game, plenty of things happen that are unexpected. But if you are playing in the long game, you'll be anchored by His Word and you'll know He has a plan that is bigger than what is happening right now. The believers who are growing, prospering and becoming who Jesus called them to be are learning to force their will to be joyful because God is bigger than anything coming at them.

My attitude is all about me. If I choose anger, I can be grumpy. I can complain, be frustrated, irritated, or discouraged. Or I can choose to be joyful. That is what the Psalmist says: I will rejoice in God. I will delight in the Lord. I will rejoice in the God of my salvation. I will. I choose. I choose. I choose. I make the decision again and again and again to choose joy.

Why choose joy? Is everything perfect? No. But He is on the throne, He is in control and He is in charge of the long game. And, in the end, we win. We win every time. We just have to choose to embrace the Word of God regardless of what we see. We have to choose to embrace the things of God regardless of what's around us. We have to choose joy.

Your attitude will dictate how long you walk through something. If your attitude is off, God is going to wait to teach you how to have a better attitude because your attitude speaks of your faith. Your attitude speaks of the depth of your relationship with the Lord. If it's off, then God needs to mature it.

It is not about what is going on around you. It is about Who is in you because greater is He that is in you than he that is in the world. Greater is His plan than this momentary bump. You need to choose joy every single day you wake up, and you need to make this a conscious decision.

I am not going to be a grumbler. I am not going to be a complainer. I am not going to be a whiner. I am not going to feel sorry for myself. I am going to check into His will and I am going to walk with joy. Child of God, if you learn to choose joy, you will be unstoppable. You become unstoppable because joy is a symbol of your faith as you walk through each day and it allows your faith to be activated. God now has the vehicle He needs to move in your life with strength.

I challenge you today to choose to be joyful. I challenge you to choose to delight in the Lord and not just to be okay, but to delight in your salvation. Be excited regardless of what is going on because God is in control.

Lets Pray: Father, I pray for all who are reading this today, that You would give them the courage to choose joy. I pray You would give them the courage, Lord God, to delight in their salvation. I pray they would not allow their circumstances to dictate their attitude, but that they would allow Your Word and Your will to dictate their attitude. Give them strength. Give them courage. Give them the ability to choose joy. In the name of Jesus! Amen!

You Can Trust God

"When we are faithless, He remains faithful
[true to His word and His righteous character],
for He cannot deny Himself."
2 Timothy 2:13 AMP

It is a pleasure to bring God's Word to you today. I will be sharing from 2 Timothy 2:13 in the Amplified Version. It says, "When we are faithless, He remains faithful, true to His word and His righteous character, for He cannot deny Himself."

There are plenty of times that we feel faithless. We cannot always see God moving. Things are going on around us and they seem purposeless, difficult, hard to understand, and we ultimately can't see God's Hand. What happens to us is we become faithless when we cannot see His Hand. We forget who He is. We forget because we are feeble. We are human and, unfortunately, our memory is short-term.

The beauty about God is that when we lose faith or when we become faithless, He continues to be faithful because He cannot deny who He is. He cannot deny His word and He cannot deny His character. He remains faithful when we become faithless.

The beauty of this is that when I cannot see God's Hand, I have to learn to trust His heart. When I cannot see Him moving in certain situations or when I don't understand what is going on around me, or when things seem confusing and out of order, as long as I recognize and remember His character, I'm going to be just fine because He will not forget who He is. I might forget because I'm a human being but God doesn't forget who He is.

His character is consistent. He is a good God. He is faithful. He is righteous. He is true. And His Word, not one word of it, will ever fall to the ground.

The B… d past time and space, the ea… will stand. Even when I becom… ıke sense to me and when things … acter and I can trust His word b… ‹ who He is. He will stay true.

have faith in God
He can do miracules
for you be patient
God has a time
for you

He is th… ıorever. He does not change. So, if He was good yesterday, He is good today and He is going to be good tomorrow. If He was faithful yesterday, He is faithful today and He is going to be faithful tomorrow. If He had my back yesterday, guess what? He will have my back today. He is going to have my back tomorrow.

All He is looking for from us is to trust His character. When we cannot see His Hand, we have to learn to trust His heart. When I don't understand why God hasn't opened the doors I think He is going to open, or hasn't shifted the things I think He needs to shift, I need to trust Him. I need to know He's in control. I need to know He is good, and that He is working all things together for good. In due season and in the right time, He is going to do what needs to happen in my life, for my family and for my future.

We serve a good God. Remember when you are faithless, when you are at the end of who you are, He remains faithful– true to His character and true to His word. We can rest in His character and we can rest in His word.

Lets Pray: Lord, help me when I can't see Your hand to trust Your Heart. Help me to remember who You are and that You are always faithful!

Open Doors

"I know your works. See, I have set before you an open door and no one can shut it, for even though you have little strength, you have kept My word and have not denied My name."
Revelations 3:8 NIV

What does it mean to live under an open heaven? There are many potential meanings to this phrase, although there is one in particular that I would like to review. Open heaven means that God can cause doors to supernaturally open. We live with many promises in our hearts and are waiting for them to come to pass. So, when we talk about an open door season, it is about the fulfillment and the manifestation of the new things that God has promised. It is about the open doors that God Himself is providing.

God is opening doors for you that no one can shut. At one point, we perceived it (this miracle), but now we will obtain the promise. God wants to open doors in your life that were previously closed. He will open them wide and will fulfill and manifest some things in your life that you have been awaiting (waiting to come to pass).

Child of God, get yourself in line with what God wants to do! Revelations 3:8 says, "I know your works. See, I have set before you an open door and no one can shut it, for even though you have little strength, you have kept My word and have not denied My name." You say, "Lord, I've been believing, I've been waiting, when is the promise coming?" Let me assure you, God honors faithfulness. He says, "You've had little strength," and we all know how it feels, at times, to have only a little strength.

"God, I can't do it," you say. But He says, "Because even in your little strength, you didn't deny my word. You didn't turn from me. You kept walking after me. Even when you were weak and feeble and had no strength, there are doors that will open in front of you that no man can shut."

I want you to receive that word into your spirit. God has opened doors for you that no man can shut because He will open them in such a way that no man can take credit. God will keep them open for as long as you need and He will make a way. All you have to do, even in your little strength is hold onto him, hold onto his word, hold onto your faith and walk in line with His word.

Let me tell you this, when we accept Jesus, it gives us access to heaven. We gain heaven when we die, but when we walk with Him, we gain heaven here on earth. When we begin to walk in His path and in obedience to His truth, heaven begins to manifest in our life. When we obey His Word and what He says, we begin to see heaven revealed on earth, which is what God desires.

He does not want you to wait until you get to heaven to experience His glory. He wants you to experience a taste of heaven every single day of your life. Settle for nothing less than this. Obey Him, walk with Him, even when you're weak. You who are of little strength, hold on. Do not deny His word or His name. Hold onto Him. The doors in front of you that will open will be unbelievable!

A few years ago, I witnessed this first hand. I had arrived at home and was preparing to go to a Vacation Bible School (VBS) I was leading. This was a new home for me as I had recently moved. It was a Friday, the end of a long week, and I was not yet accustomed to my locks or keys. As I was preparing to go, I accidentally locked myself out of the garage.

My thoughts were, "I've got to go to work. I don't have time to figure this out. When I come home, I'll just go through the front door and then put my car into the garage." So, I left for work, ran the VBS, sent everyone home, grabbed something to eat, and finally arrived back at home at one thirty in the morning. I was accompanied by a young girl who was staying with me at the time while she was assisting us at Vacation Bible School. As I approached my front door, I realized that I didn't have the key to the screen door. I had a key for the front door but I couldn't open the screen door.

As I stood there baffled, not really sure what to do, the young girl started looking around for an open window. I had to explain to her that since I am originally from New York, there was NO CHANCE of an unlocked window. They were all bolted shut. I began looking around trying to figure out what to do. I did not know who to call at that moment and, finally, decided to break the handle. I was going to put all my force on the handle, break it, and let myself in.

Well, as I put all my force on the handle to the screen door, I realized that it was not attached to the lock, it was purely decorative. At that point, I just lifted up my hands before the Lord. I was tired! It had been a long day of ministry. In my exhaustion, I lifted my hands and said, "Lord, I need your help. I don't know what to do."

Family, God as my witness - I looked at the lock, and in front of my eyes, it turned by itself! All by itself!! It turned and the young lady that was with me looked and said, "Did I just see that lock turn?"

I said, "Yeah, so did I."

She exclaimed, "Is the door unlocked?!"

I said "There is only one way to find out," so I turned the handle and opened the door. The door that was completely dead-bolted a second before was now open! As I opened the door, I heard the Spirit of the Lord say to me, "When I want to open a door for my child, no one holds Me back. When I am ready to open up a door for My child, there is not a door that I cannot open, there is not a deadbolt that I cannot get through, there is not a chain I cannot break. When I am ready to open a door for my child, no man will stop Me."

I have to tell you that verse, that word, is now embedded in my spirit. When God is moving and He opens doors, no man can shut them. I want you to sit on the seat of expectation of open doors. God's got it for you and I want you to grab hold of these words. Grab hold and pray them through. I want you to cry them out before God. Push for them and, even though you may feel weak, don't deny His word. Don't deny His name and remember what the Lord said to this church: "I remember that even though you were weak, you did not deny My name, you did not deny My Word and I will open doors for you that no man can shut." He says the same to you, grab a hold of that today, and walk in it.

Lets Pray: Father, I declare over every person today in the name of Jesus, I speak grace, power, and open doors. I ask for the fulfillment and manifestation of Your promises. God, give them courage in their weakness, to hold onto Your word and stand fast because You promised You will open doors that no man can shut. Lord, we give it to You and we say, "Have Your way." In Jesus' name, amen.

Walk in the Spirit

"Walk in the spirit
and you will not fulfill the lust of the flesh."
Galatians 5:16 NKJV

Oftentimes, I get asked questions about how to overcome a particular sin that has been a struggle or how to find victory in a certain situation. Some will say, "I don't know how to stop being angry," "I don't know how to forgive," or "how to stop doing what offends God." We often spend so much time focusing on a particular sin, not realizing that the scripture has given us an answer. Galatians 5:16 says, "Walk in the spirit and you will not fulfill the lust of the flesh." It seems like a very simple statement, but what does it mean to walk in the Spirit? What does it mean to have that daily communion with the Holy Spirit? Well, it is exactly that.

As I begin my morning meditating on God's Word and sitting with the Holy Spirit, I allow Him to have access into every area of my life. I often hear people say they want more of the Holy Spirit. But, the bottom line is, we do not need more of the Holy Spirit, He needs more of us. We have to create more room in our lives for the Holy Spirit to fill. We must allow Him more access to who we are, how we think, function and live.

As we give the Holy Spirit more room in these areas, we'll find that the things that were always a struggle, troublesome, burdensome, or possibly even chains in our lives, will begin to fall off. As we walk in the Spirit, we will not fulfill the lust of the flesh for this is a byproduct of walking in the Spirit.

Take your focus off of your sin or mistakes. Focus on the Lord. Look to the Spirit of the Lord and begin to seek Him out. The Bible says that in every temptation, the Lord will give you a way of escape. What does that mean? If you lean on Him, when temptation and struggles come, He will give you a way out. He will give you a way to think and function at a higher level than what you could achieve on your own.

The Bible says His ways are much higher than our ways. His way of thinking is much higher than our way. But we will never know it unless we walk by the Spirit, unless we pray in the Spirit, and unless we sit with the Spirit. As He was leaving the earth, Jesus said, "I'm sending you One who is the same as Me, the Holy Spirit."

What did He mean by that?

Having the Spirit of God is the same as having Jesus. Now it is not just one person walking the earth, but the Spirit of God that walks in tandem with you daily as he continuously fills every crevice of who you are and who I am. Therefore, if we give Him access and space, we will find that our lives will change.

Child of God, walk in the Spirit, pray in the Spirit, live in the Spirit, and you will not fulfill the lust of the flesh.

Lets Pray: I pray for you in the name of Jesus, proclaiming His grace over you. May He grant you anointing, power, and a deep understanding of the things of the Spirit. I pray in His mighty name that you will walk in the Spirit and watch your life change dramatically. Grace to you, in Jesus name. Amen!

The Lord Before Me

"I've put the Lord before me always.
And because He is at my right hand,
I shall not be moved."
Psalm 16:8 NIV

Each day, God has a fresh word for you and today is no different. Today's word is found in Psalm 16:8. It says, "I've put the Lord before me always. And because He is at my right hand, I shall not be moved." You might say, "Oh, that's a really simple scripture," but it's actually not. The Lord wants us to recognize that whatever we put in the forefront determines our response, and ultimately, our destiny.

Whatever I put in front of me determines how I respond and where I will go. And so, the Psalmist writes, "I've put the Lord always before me." Why? "Because He is at my right hand, I shall not be moved."

You see family, whatever we put in front of us, whatever we focus on and set our eyes on, these are the things that will affect our responses and reactions. If we put doctors or the pressures of work in front of us, these will be the things that move us. That is why the scripture is clear: we are to always put the Lord in front of us.

If my eyes are always on the Lord, He is at my right hand, everything around me can shake, but I will not be shaken because He is able to keep me steady. If He is before me as my guide, I will not be moved from His purpose for my life. If He is always in front leading me, He will be able to warn me of mistakes and missteps. However, if I am looking all around and not focused on Him, I can be led in any direction.

So, my questions for you today, child of God, what have you put in front of you? What are you looking toward? Where is your focus? The scripture is clear that He must increase and everything else must decrease. If He is increasing, then we are not moved. However, if other things are increasing, we will be shaken. Our emotions will be up and down, and when our fears are forward, our faith falls back. However, if He is in front of us, we shall not be moved.

Lets Pray: Today, I pray in the name of Jesus that God will touch you. I pray in the name of Jesus that He would meet you. I pray that He would be magnified in your life, and that you, child of God, will keep the Lord ever before you, so you will not be moved. Have an amazing day, and may God bless you as you walk in His favor.

It is Time to Prophesy!

I want to share something that burns in my heart, and it's not necessarily a scripture but a biblical principle that's taught throughout the word of God. It's the idea that the children of God have been called to live prophetic lives.

Do you know that you are a supernatural being? You are not an earthly being. You might walk on Planet Earth, but the Bible says we are in the world, but not of the world. We are supernatural beings that have been bought by the blood of Jesus. The spirit of God lives in us, and we have been called to live prophetic lives.

Now, what do I mean by that?

Oftentimes, we get confused because we think: "I'm not called to be a prophet. Prophets fall under a very specific office." That is true. However, there is a very specific office of the prophet referred to in the bible. Take me for example, I have a personal calling to be a pastor, that is the office I sit in. Although, this does not mean that you, as a child of God, cannot be pastoral yourself. It does not mean that you cannot care for the body or teach. You just may not sit in that office. However, everyone has been called to serve in the ministry and to serve in the things of God.

In the Word of God, we find prophets like Ezekiel and Jeremiah. These were prophets of God, and there are even modern-day prophets like David Wilkerson. These are prophets that sit in that office. But, child of God, every single one of us has been called to prophesy.

What exactly does that mean?

Prohesy means to take the word of God and prophetically speak it over your life and your circumstances. A prophet speaks God's heart out loud. A person in the office of the prophet hears God and speaks. We have sixty-six books in the Bible, and so our job is to live out these words, and begin to speak His word prophetically.

When do we do this? When we face an impossible situation. What does Jesus say to his disciples in the book of Matthew? He says, "Anyone who speaks to the mountain and tells it to move, it will move." What is He really telling them? He's telling them, prophesy, speak my word and the mountain is going to move. What does He tell other people? He says, "Speak this out and watch it come to pass." He tells Ezekiel, "Prophesy to the bones, prophesy to the wind." In other words, He is saying, "Speak my word out loud."

Child of God, you need to understand that you are called to live a prophetic life. Do not declare your own words or speak your words. Our words are nonsense and they have no life in them. What does have life is the word of God. The Bible says it is a living, breathing and acting organism. It breaths, and when we take God's word and speak it out loud and speak it over our circumstances, we will see things change.

We are called to prophesy and speak life. For example, when your child is acting crazy, don't call them crazy. When a child is not behaving, don't speak death over them, speak life over them. Is your marriage a mess? Speak life over it. Is your own health a mess? Speak life. Begin to declare the word of God over your body, over your mind, over your church and over your circumstances. Begin to prophesy, and begin to speak out His word with clarity and power.

What is the first step? You have to know His word. You have to absorb it, and then begin to let it come out of your mouth. The

Bible says, faith comes by hearing and hearing by the word of God. Your faith will grow as you begin to speak the word of God out loud.

Don't accept the lies of the enemy. Don't even accept your reasoning, for your reasoning has to be subject to the Word of God. Your reasoning is subject to the things of God, not your life experience. All of those things need to come under the word of God, and we as the children of God need to speak prophetically. We need to begin to speak His word out loud.

We can't get caught up in our circumstances or situations. We need to be the supernatural people that God has called us to be. The children of God have been called to live extraordinary lives. We're not meant to live humdrum, automatic, go to work, come home lives. We were meant to live lives full of the prophetic fire of Jesus!

Do not settle for anything less. Not a C+, a B or even a good A minus. Go for everything God has for you. Prophesy over your life, speak His word! As you speak, continue to speak words of faith. Speak over your health, marriage and over your church. Be that persistent voice of God and watch what happens. Just as when Ezekiel watched in the Valley of the dry bones, the bones all came together, and eventually they came to life.

God Himself breathed into those old bones and produced life, and He will do the same in your circumstances as you stand by faith. That is what prophecy is: standing by faith. We cannot believe only our circumstances, but stand on the Word of God. Stand by faith, speak it out, and God Himself will breathe into it.

Lets Pray: I prophesy over you today in the name of Jesus. I declare life and strength, refreshing and peace. I pray right now in the name of Jesus that He would breathe His life into you. That you would sense His power and His pulling, and that you would learn as His child to speak His word with power, authority

and passion. You have no need to fear anything because truly, God is for us.

The Heart of the King

"The king's heart is in the hand of the Lord.
Like the rivers of water,
He turns it wherever He wishes."
Proverbs 21:1 NKJV

Proverbs 21:1 tells us that the heart of the King is in the hands of the Lord and like water, He turns it any way that He wishes. What does that mean? It means that God holds all things in His hands. Nothing is outside of His sight and like water, He turns it any way that He wants. He turns it any way that He sees fit.

The Bible says that we are blessed and highly favored. We need to remember that and call it out in our lives. There are times when we walk into situations and what we need is Godly favor. Or we need God to show up. At those times, we need to say, "God, the heart of the King is in Your hands, turn it toward me God, turn it toward favor, turn it toward what I need or what I'm looking for Lord God. You control all things. Give me favor."

A boy in one of the youth groups that I pastored years ago had an issue at school. The situation looked terrible and he was going to be expelled. He had gone through three appeals and it still did not look promising. We prayed all night. I kept speaking out that the heart of the King would turn in favor towards him. The next day, he met with the final appeal court. The person that was in charge walked over to him and said, "I don't know who you are but all night, my heart was turning." (Did you hear that?) "All night, my heart was turning and I shouldn't give you a second chance, but I'm going to give you a second chance."

You know what? He didn't turn his own heart. God turned his heart. The Bible says that the heart of the King is in the hands of the Lord and He turns it any way that He wants. Know today, that when you're walking into a circumstance or situation, you can pray beforehand for the heart of the King to be turned. You can pray for the circumstance to work out in your favor. You should make it a practice to pray before you walk into any situation, before you begin any discussion, that God would govern and rule and turn the situation in your favor.

There are many challenges in front of us, as individuals, as well as the Church, that need the favor of God. We have to pray for God to put His Hands over them. We need divine wisdom and creativity in order to navigate the things that are in front of us. We need the heart of the king to turn!

Lets Pray: I pray for the heart of the King to turn in favor towards the things that are right and the things that are Godly. Today, I declare you blessed child of God. I declare you highly favored and I thank You Lord that the heart of the King is in your hands and that you turn it towards your people! Amen!

Be Strong and of Good Courage

"Have I not commanded you? Be strong and of good courage;
do not be afraid, nor be dismayed,
for the Lord your God is with you wherever you go."
Joshua 1:9 NKJV

I want to share with you from Joshua, one of my favorite books in the Bible. I love the spirit of Joshua. I love the heart of Joshua. In Joshua chapter one, God is instructing Joshua, now that he is leading the people of Israel. Moses has died, and He is preparing Joshua to be his successor. As He is preparing him, God begins to give Joshua some instructions as to how they are going to step in and take the Promised Land.

Remember, Moses led them to the border, but he did not lead them all the way inside. Joshua was the one that brought Israel to the Promised Land. As Joshua approached the last major steps that needed to take place to possess the Promised Land, the Lord tells him, "Joshua, be strong, be of good courage. I am going to give you every place that you put your foot. Don't move from the left or the right. Keep the law I put in front of you, walk strong, meditate on it and you will prosper. Just keep My word in your heart." And then He tells him again, "Be strong and of good courage. I am going to be with you. I am not going to leave you. I'll never forsake you."

God continues to speak into Joshua as we come to today's verse - Joshua 1:9. "Have I not commanded you? Be strong and be of good courage. Do not be afraid, nor be dismayed, for the Lord your God is with you wherever you go." It is very interesting that the Lord says to Joshua three times, "be strong, be of good courage." But before the third time he adds, "Have I not commanded you?" We don't talk about that verse very often, but the Lord is actually giving him a command.

He must be strong and of good courage. It was not an option, it was not a choice. It was not something that he could kind of maybe have and maybe not have. If Joshua was going to be who God called him to be, and if he was going to walk into the things God had prepared for him, strength and courage were not options. They were a command. Child of God, anything that you want to accomplish for God, anything that you want to accomplish in your life, anything that you want to be, if you want to be who Jesus called you to be, being strong and being courageous are not options.

You must be strong and of good courage. He has commanded you to be these things. And the reason you can be strong and the reason you can have courage is the portion right after. "Do not be afraid, do not be dismayed for the Lord your God will go with you wherever you go."

Do you know, child of God, that you never walk alone? You are never alone. You might feel alone, but that is a lie from the enemy. You are never alone. The Lord Jesus walks with you every moment of every day and because He walks with you, you don't have to be afraid. You do not have to be dismayed. You can be strong. You can be courageous. As a matter of fact, God Himself commands you to be strong and be courageous.

Do that today. Do it this week. Do it always! Remind yourself, "has He not commanded me to be strong and of good courage? Has He told me not to be afraid, not to be dismayed because He is going to be with me wherever I go?"

What land do you need to possess this week? What Jerichos

do you need to walk around this week and take authority over? What is it that you need strength for? Remind yourself, "God has given me a mandate and I am going to take it. I am going to be strong and of good courage. I am not going to be afraid. I am not going to be dismayed, because the Lord God is going to go with me wherever I go. I never walk alone."

Be encouraged and be the champion God has called you to be. Be strong and of good courage, child of God. Possess the land in front of you. Walk in victory and walk in everything God has for you, do not be afraid, do not be dismayed for the Lord goes with you everywhere you go.

Lets Pray: Father, I pray that Your people would be filled with courage, that they would not allow fear to hold them back! I pray they would stand in their rightful place as Your children with their heads high, knowing that they never walk alone. Give them the courage to walk around every mountain that comes before them and make it fall! Amen!

That's Too Small

"Now to him who is able to do exceedingly abundantly more than you could hope or imagine through the power of Christ at work in us."
Ephesians 3:20 NIV

I love sharing the word of God. I truly get so excited! I want to share with you one of my favorite verses. It's found in the book of Ephesians. Ephesians 3:20 says, "Now to him who is able to do exceedingly abundantly more than you could hope or imagine through the power of Christ at work in us." I love this verse, and most times we just quote the beginning, "to him who is able to do exceedingly abundantly more than we could hope or imagine." Right? But we don't finish it off. It's through the power of Christ that's at work in us and through us.

See, God is able to do more than we can ever dream. Oftentimes, when we're dreaming about things, I can almost hear God saying, "You're dreaming too little. I have more, I have much more." Yet, sometimes, we think of God as being like a genie. He pops out the 'exceedingly abundantly more than we could hope or imagine', to fulfill our wish. However, it is not that simple. It's with the power of Christ that's working in us. What that means is that as I walk with God and as I'm allowing His spirit to work in me and to have His way in me, I've now set the stage for the 'exceedingly abundantly more than I can hope or imagine.'

See, if I think God is like a genie, that I can just ask Him and He'll give me the 'exceedingly abundantly more' without any connection, that would be very wrong. God works within relationship. God works with His people as He walks with His people. Today, I want you to understand that as you walk with Christ, as you connect with Him, as you allow His spirit to work in you and through you, what happens is the "exceedingly abundantly more."

As you're walking out your life with God, the "exceedingly abundantly more" becomes more than you could imagine and more than you could think. God is not only present when you need Him or when you call Him. He also cares for us when we're far from him. He does because He is a good father.

However, I want the 'exceedingly abundantly more than I can hope or imagine" every day. I don't want it simply when I'm in trouble. I don't want it when I'm desperate; I want to walk in the 'exceedingly abundant' every single day of my life. The way to walk into the "exceedingly abundantly more than you can hope or imagine" is by allowing the power of Christ to work in you and through you.

See, God is at work in our life. If we allow him to have a place, if we allow him to expand in us, and we allow him to work in us, then the 'exceedingly abundantly more than we can hope or imagine' becomes the byproduct. You walk in favor when you walk with God. Favor is part of who God is and favor has everything to do with how you're walking before the Lord. As you walk with Him, favor becomes part of who you are. God favors His people. And so, it is part of the 'exceedingly abundant' that God wants to pour over you, but He pours it over you as you walk with Him.

So, I want to encourage you to stay close to God. I want you to begin to live a life of expectation. Ask yourself, "What am I expecting?"– The exceedingly abundantly. "What am I looking for?" – God to show up. When you expect for God to show up, don't expect him to show up a little bit, expect him to show up big. God wants to show up big and He wants a people that have the faith to believe for the big.

Remember, you won't have the faith to believe for the big unless you spend time with a big God. See it all goes together. When I spend time with God and he becomes a big God to me, then I have no problem believing Him for big things because I know Him. He's at work in me and as He's at work in me, believing Him for big things becomes easy because I know how big He is. I know how big He is today, and tomorrow He'll be even bigger because every day I get to know God better.

You can know a big God today. As you continue to spend time with Him daily, you'll see how magnified His presence will become in your life. As you continue to seek His presence, you'll begin to see the "exceedingly abundantly more than we could hope or imagine." God wants to blow your mind, child of God. Get close to Him so you can live every day in the expectation of God's goodness. Trust that He has His best for you, and that His plan is bigger than what you could imagine.

Lets Pray: I pray for those reading today. I pray they would allow you to work in them and through them, Lord God, and as they do that, Father, I declare the 'exceedingly abundantly more than they can hope or imagine' would show up for them. God, let them wake up every morning with the expectation of "God, what are you going to do today? How are you going to blow my mind today, Lord God?" I pray that you would anoint them and cover them. I pray that you would draw them close, and you would make a way for them. Open up the doors that need to be open and close the doors that need to be closed. Father, open the doors that no man can open. Anoint them, I pray. Bless them. Walk with them. Make yourself real to them in every way, Lord God. I declare blessings over every one of them, in Jesus name. Amen.

Healing Belongs to the Household of Faith

"Bless the Lord, oh my soul, and forget not all His benefits, who forgives all your sins and heals all your diseases."
Psalms 103:2-3 NKJV

Each of us receives fresh grace or, as I like to say, fresh manna, to walk out whatever comes our way on a given day. God gave you the grace when you opened your eyes today to face whatever would be coming your way. With this in mind, take a look at Psalms 103:2-3 which reads, "Bless the Lord, oh my soul, and forget not all His benefits, who forgives all your sins and heals all your diseases." I love this verse because our God does things completely, never just half way.

When He begins a good work, He finishes what He starts. When Jesus went to the cross of Calvary, the Bible says that He defeated the enemy. It even says that He made a public spectacle of him. It says that He destroyed Satan's works. He also destroyed the grave and the power of sin over your life.

Child of God, there is no sin today that can hold you. Jesus has delivered you of all of it, and there is no sin you could commit today that the Father could not forgive. His Word says that He forgives all of our sins! Our job is to confess our sins to the Lord and repent. The word repentance means to turn and to return.

And so I turn from that sin, I acknowledge it before God, and I turn back to God. And as I do that, God forgives me, takes my sin and casts it as far as the East is from the West and will never hold it against me. Once I repent, He cleanses me and gives me a brand new day.

Same is true for healing. The Word says He heals all my diseases. We, sometimes, step away from this word because people do not always get healed. Right now, I want to stick to the word where the Bible says that Jesus has defeated all sickness, all disease. There is nothing that He cannot heal, and there is nothing He is not willing to heal. The Bible says that He has healed all our diseases.

So, I don't know what you are struggling with in your body today. I don't know what sickness is upon you or what you struggle with in your mind. There are those that are struggling with things in their joints and in their physical body. Even things with sleep and many other things, sometimes as simple as a migraine headache. We tolerate them, and Jesus is saying, "Why would you tolerate them? I've delivered you from all of that. Sickness is not part of what I want for you. The inheritance of a child of God is healing." And so, we believe God for healing, for forgiveness of all sin, all bondage being broken from your life.

We need to take God at His word. He said, "I have forgiven all sin and healed all diseases." So, we come to Him in simple faith, and we should not complicate it or overthink it. We can say, "I need deliverance and I need healing." And you know what else you can do? The Bible even says you can stand in proxy for someone.

What does that mean?

Maybe you're not physically sick, but you know somebody that is. Stand in their place and say, "Lord, I'm going to cry out for so-and-so who needs healing in their body, and I'm going to believe You to touch them. I believe You already have at the cross of Calvary." The Bible says that by His stripes we are healed and made whole. We have been delivered from sickness. Deliverance and healing belong to the household of faith.

So I am going to pray for you and if you are sick in your body, or know someone that is sick, or if there's a sin that has been a struggle, we are going to believe that we will remember the benefits of the Lord and all that Jesus did on the cross. We will receive it today with faith and with authority as His children, knowing that Jesus has done a great work.

As we pray, if you feel healing flow through your body, I want you to email me. Please contact me at www.marshamansour.com and let me know!! It is so encouraging to hear that God is at work, and I have already received several testimonies of God's miraculous healing. There was a woman who was having a miscarriage and God spontaneously stopped the miscarriage. Unbelievable things have occurred that people have emailed to us, and we are so excited, but we want more!

We believe God is in the healing and delivering business. So if you are sick in body, you know someone that is, if you know someone that's in bondage, we're going to take Jesus at His word and receive healing today.

Lets Pray: Father, we give You praise. We give You honor. We thank You God that at the cross of Calvary You delivered, You set free, and You broke the work of the enemy. Today, in Jesus' name, I pray that You would extend Your hand right now. Father, I pray for every person that is reading this today, and I declare healing over their physical body. We come against whatever is going on with them. Every ailment, every sickness, cancer, diabetes, fibromyalgia, heart issue, Lupus, dementia, Alzheimer's – Father, I come against every bit of it. All these diseases that they say have no cure. You are the cure, Jesus. And so, we extend our faith today knowing that You are able.

We curse these diseases and we speak healing over all that are reading today, from the top of their head to the soles of their feet. We command healing to flow in them right now and may they be miraculously healed Lord, as they extend their faith and believe You today. May they take You at your word Lord.

And Father, I pray for those that are struggling with sin. Father, I thank You that sin was broken at the cross of Calvary. And today, Lord, may they walk in the freedom that You have for them. Touch them with liberty today, Lord God. Your Word is clear, 'whom the Son has set free, is free indeed'.

And so we declare liberty and freedom, God, that nothing would hold them or tie them down. They would walk in all that You have for them, Lord. Bless the Lord, oh my soul, all that is within me! We will not forget your benefits Lord. You are a good and faithful God. We love You Father. May Your presence be sweet to those that read this Lord, and may You lead and walk with them every moment. For Your glory in Jesus name. Amen.

Stone Upon Stone

What I want to share with you is not a verse, but a story. A story to help you understand a principle that God shows us in His Word in the book of Joshua. Moses has died and Joshua has been put in charge of Israel. As the Israelites are preparing to enter the Promised Land, they come up to another river they have to cross. They all remember the Red Sea.

Now, they approach the Jordan River and God parts the waters again! But there is a difference this time. At the Red Sea, God parted the waters before they stepped into it. Crossing the Jordan River was going to be different. God brought them to the Jordan River at high tide, and they had to walk in it. They had to get into the water. Once they began to step into the water, God parted the sea.

He parted it the same way He did the Red Sea, but the behavior of Israel was different. The step of faith was different. When they came out of Egypt and came up to the Red Sea, they were babies in the faith. So God spoon fed them. He parted the Red Sea before they ever had to take a step of faith.

Now, they're ready to enter the Promised Land. They approach the Jordan River, but now the requirement of faith is different. He's not going to spoon feed them. He now requires them to act upon the faith they've grown in during their time in the wilderness.

Many of you are walking through the wilderness and you are trying to figure out why you are walking through this. A huge portion of the answer is that your muscle of faith is being stretched. So, as it's being flexed and being stretched, and being flexed and being stretched, you're going to come up to a valley like this.

A Jordan River is going to be in front of you and God's not going to part it right away. He's going to require you to walk a little bit into the water at high tide. The Israelites walked into the Jordan at high tide. The water was high and it was moving. God made them walk out, not one step or two steps. The scripture says He made them walk out to the middle of the river.

It wasn't until they got out to the middle of the Jordan River that He parted it. They had to trust Him that they weren't going to get swept up in the waves. They had to trust Him that the water wasn't going to overcome them. They had to trust Him that He was going to show up for them – and He did.

Scripture is clear that those who trust in the Lord will never be put to shame. When we exercise faith, God never allows us to be put to shame. So. they went. They stepped out into the middle of the river, God parted it and they walked across.

But then God gives them a simple little instruction. He says, "Pick up stones from the dry land, where I've parted the sea. Pick up stones and take them with you, and set them up as an altar when you get to the Promised Land."

You say, "What are those stones for?"

Well, the scripture calls them remembrance stones. They were stones the Israelites were to put down at the altar for them to remember God's faithfulness. They were still going to have to fight many enemies: the Canaanites, the Ammonites and all the enemies that came after that. By looking at those stones, God wanted them to remember that He was faithful and He was going to be there.

Child of God, the only thing that prepares you for the battle that's going to come tomorrow is remembering the victory that came yesterday. I want to say that again. The only thing that's going to prepare you for the battle of tomorrow is the victory that came yesterday. I live in this place. You and I live in this place where every day we're going to meet a battle. What throws us off is when we stop remembering the goodness of God. We never have to worry about what's going to happen because we have a history with God of His faithfulness, goodness and righteousness that we can tap into.

So we can say, "Wait, God, you've shown up before. You've been faithful before. I can trust you." You see Israel could walk into the Jordan River because they had the Red Sea. He parted the Red Sea. Now, God said, "Okay, now remember that? I'll do it again." Once they left the Jordan, they ended up in Jericho and they had to believe again, and again.

Each time the requirement is more - much more, because God is looking for people that are going to trust Him. And the way to walk in trust, the way to develop faith is to live in the victory of each day and say, "God, I remember what You did yesterday. I remember what You did before. I trust You. You've been faithful. You're not going to allow me to be put to shame." Each time God shows up.

So, we have these remembrance stones. Maybe they are stones, or maybe there's something you remember in your heart. I know for me it was when I took a trip to Florida and as I was walking on the sand, God spoke to me. He spoke to me so clearly and concisely. What God said was so overwhelming that I actually brought sand home with me. I brought a whole big bag of sand home with me from Florida! Another time, I was in the Caribbean and God did it again. And so I brought home sand!

You're like, "I think, well, she's crazy. Why is she carrying sand?" It's because it was a moment when God showed up and I wanted to remember it. So now, every time I look at it, every time I put it in my hand and touch it, I say, "God, I remember Your faithfulness. I remember how You've spoken, God. I remember that You are God and God alone. You showed up for my Red Sea. You showed up for my Jordan. You showed up for my Jericho and You're going to show up for every single battle that's going to come."

What's going to prepare you for the battle that comes tomorrow is the victory of today, and you are going to take remembrance stones and place them deep in your heart. You are going to build your faith one stone upon one stone upon one stone, and you are going to take every victory as it comes knowing that you serve a faithful God.

Lets Pray: And so Father, I thank You God that we all have a history of Your faithfulness and of Your goodness. Lord, we build our faith rock upon rock and stone upon stone. Father, whether You're going to part the Red Sea before we step in, or You're going to part the sea as we step in, God, either way, we know that You're going to show up and part the sea. And so, we trust You, God. We exercise our muscles of faith, believing that You are exactly who You say You are, Lord God. We remember Your goodness. We remember Your faithfulness, Lord God, and we know that as we step forward, You will never allow us to be put to shame. Amen.

Surrounded by Him

"As the mountain surrounds Jerusalem, so the Lord surrounds His people from this time forth and forever. For the scepter of the wicked shall not rest on the land allotted to the righteous."
Psalms 125:2-3 NKJV

There is a word that was planted in my heart so strongly by the Lord. It is found in Psalms 125. Starting at verse 2, it says, "As the mountain surrounds Jerusalem, so the Lord surrounds His people from this time forth and forevermore, for the scepter of the wicked shall not rest on the land allotted to the righteous." I love this verse because it was written during a time when Israel felt surrounded and the Lord said, "Don't worry. The same way the mountains surround Jerusalem, (because Jerusalem is embedded with mountains all around) so the Lord surrounds His people." The Lord makes a circle around His people from this day forevermore.

That includes us!

While this might've been written in the time of David, it extends beyond. The Lord says from this point forth and forever, He surrounds His people so that the scepter of the wicked does not rest on the land allotted to the righteous. The scepter of the wicked are the plans of the enemy, or the things that he wants to do to harm us or to hurt us. The Bible says the scepter of the wicked will not rest on the land allotted to the righteous. Why? Because the Lord surrounds his people. The Lord surrounding his people deters the scepter of the wicked from being placed on the land allotted to the righteous.

Child of God, I want to encourage you that whatever you are walking through, the Lord surrounds you. There's this beautiful worship song. It says that you might feel like you're surrounded, but all you are surrounded with is the Lord. And that's the truth. It doesn't matter what's coming at you. It only matters who's around you. And the Lord is saying the same way the mountains surround Jerusalem, so the Lord Himself surrounds you, child of God.

You are surrounded by the Lord. He has you covered on every end, and the scepter of the wicked cannot rest on the land allotted to the righteous. When I started in the ministry, I was in my early teens. At 17 or 18, I was working in youth ministry. Every Friday night after service, I would drive a whole bunch of teenagers home. At the time, I was a poor kid in Bible school. In Bible school, you had no money for gas. You had no money for anything! Often, I wouldn't have enough gas to take them home. It would be a 40 minute drive and the youth feared they were going to end up pushing the car. I would just quote this verse over and over in my car. I would say, "Lord, I thank You that the scepter of the wicked will not rest on the land allotted to the righteous. Lord, I am Your child and You surround me." And so the Lord would meet us every time! Listen to me. Every time, I made it. My car never stopped. And I promise you, there was not a drop of gas in that car. It was all fumes. God was so faithful.

It doesn't matter what seems to be surrounding us. It matters what truly is surrounding us. The Lord says, "I surround you, I am with you now and forevermore, and I surround you. I cover you on every area. And the scepter of the wicked will not rest on the land I've given you." Anything that belongs to a child of God, the scepter of the wicked cannot rest on. Anything that God has given us, the scepter of the wicked cannot have.

And that literally means anything: your home, your job, your children, or your property. Anything. The scepter of the wicked cannot rest on the land allotted to the righteous. And if it tries to rest, it's criminal, and you have to treat it like a criminal. You rebuke it. You say, "This land belongs to the righteous. You are not allowed here."

You take your authority as a child of God and say, "The scepter of the wicked cannot rest on the land allotted to the righteous." You may say, "Well, I'm the righteous?" Absolutely, you are. The Bible declares you righteous. The day you gave your life to Jesus, the blood of Jesus washed you and now you have become the righteousness of God. So you can stand in that authority; you can stand in that identity today knowing that the Lord Himself surrounds you and that if the scepter of the wicked tries to rest on you, it has no place. It has no authority and you can rebuke it and move it out.

And so I want to encourage you. You might feel surrounded today, but know that it's the Lord that surrounds you, the same way He surrounds the mountains of Jerusalem. He surrounds His children from now and forevermore. There is not a time you are alone. There is not a time when you are by yourself. He is always around you. And the scepter of the wicked cannot rest on the things that are allotted to you, child of God.

Lets Pray: Lord God, I thank you for Your grace over those that are reading. I pray God, You would bless them, You would anoint them, and You would walk with them. God, I pray that they would know that You surround them, Lord God, that You are always around them, Lord God, and that the scepter of the wicked cannot rest on the land that You've given to them. And Father, I pray that they would remember that it doesn't matter what it looks like around them; all that matters is what truly is around them, and that's You, Lord. We bless you, In Jesus' Name. Amen.

Weighty Words

"In a multitude of words, sin is not far.
But he who restrains his lips is wise."
Proverbs 10:19 NIV

I want to share an interesting verse with you found in the book of Proverbs. Proverbs 10:19 says, "In a multitude of words, sin is not far. But he who restrains his lips is wise." It's so easy to speak all the time. It's very easy to talk, to share opinions, to say things, and talk constantly. But this scripture is saying that talking all the time is not the best thing. In a multitude of words, when you talk without thinking, when you talk all the time, when you talk without listening, the Bible says, "sin is not far."

You're going to make a mistake. You're going to say something you don't mean. You're going to say something you haven't thought about. You're going to say something that just came off the top of your head that you didn't process properly. You're going to say something the Holy Spirit didn't get a chance to filter.

The Bible says, "In a multitude of words, sin is not far." Not only your words, but your conversation: a multitude of conversation, lighthearted conversation, gossip, backbiting, bad mouthing. Those things are not far. Sin is not far when saying something you don't mean: exaggerating, lying. In a multitude of words, sin is not far.

How many times are you in a conversation and find yourself saying, "I shouldn't have said that?" But you said it because you got caught up in a multitude of words. And the Bible says, "In that, sin is not far. But he who restrains his lips is wise." Be the person who knows when to speak and when not to speak.

Silence is a very powerful gift. Silence is a great, great way to keep from sinning. There's another verse that says, "Even a fool is considered wise when he doesn't speak." "Even a fool is considered wise when he's quiet." And so, there is a great strength in being quiet. There's great strength in learning how to listen and not always speak.

When you learn to restrain your lips, don't say everything you think, don't say everything that comes into your mind, you can learn to be led by Holy Spirit. Learn to be led of God.

"Father, should I say this? Lord, is this appropriate? Is it going to benefit anybody?" If your words are not going to build, don't speak them. The Bible says, "The power of life and death is in your tongue." So, if your words are not going to breathe life, don't speak them because in that is sin. When we speak and it's not led of the Lord, or we speak foolishly, or speak down to anybody or about anybody, it's ungodly. God doesn't honor that. He's saying, "In a multitude of words, sin is not far." You will make a mistake. But learn, child of God, to restrain your lips and to speak only when necessary.

I was preaching at a church and I said this simple sentence, "Don't speak a lot, but when you speak, make it powerful." You don't have to speak every moment. But when you speak, let your words be weighty so that it becomes a place where people can hear God, even in your words, even in your laugh. It's okay to joke. It's okay to be lighthearted. It's okay to be gregarious. All of those are wonderful qualities to possess. But you want to be careful that you don't get so caught up in your conversation, you find yourself saying things you shouldn't.

You want to make sure your words are weighty, so they have power and they have potency, and they have the ability for God to use. But if you just speak and never restrain your mouth, you find yourself in a mess.

In a multitude of words, sin is not far. Make sure that when you speak, you speak with words that are weighty, words that are godly, and words that breathe life. Learn to restrain your mouth. Don't say everything that comes to your mind. Learn to be led of the Spirit so that what you say is not damaging, but what you say is life-giving and anointed. Let's learn, as the Bible says, to control our tongue because by far it is the hardest thing for us to learn to control.

Lets Pray: Father, I pray that You teach those reading how to restrain their lips, Lord God, so that they speak words that are life-giving, words that are encouraging, words that are strengthening. Teach us that in a multitude of words, sin is not far. Help us not to speak all the time, every moment. But when we speak, let it be words of value. Let us be people that know how to use our words to give life and not take life. Teach us to train our tongues so that our tongues are godly and they bring You glory. In Jesus' Name. Amen.

The Trust is in the Waiting

"My soul waits in silence for the Lord alone, in Him is my expectation."
Psalms 62:5 NIV

W-A-I-T is the four letter word in Christianity. No one likes to wait! As a matter of fact, we hate it! However, there is great power in waiting. In Psalms 62:5, it says, "My soul waits in silence for the Lord alone, in Him is my expectation." We as believers hate the word wait because we think that waiting is a form of punishment, but it really is not.

Wait is wait. Wait. And what wait means is God saying, "I'm working this out for you. Just wait, trust Me." And in the waiting, God is teaching you trust. In the waiting, God is orchestrating things. You just don't know it because you are unable to see it. Still, God says, "Wait on Me."

There is actually a command here in what David wrote. He said, "My soul waits for the Lord alone in silence." What he's saying is I chose to trust God and not move ahead of Him, which is our natural instinct. We are not to lose hope and fall behind, but just to wait because our expectation is in Him alone.

You know, a lot of times we put our expectation in man, or in circumstances, or maybe even in ourselves. But scripture is telling us, don't put your expectation in anything but the Lord. Believe God to be God.

May I tell you something? You are not waiting for your outcome! We often lose heart in waiting for God because we don't get the outcome that we wanted. And then we say, "Well, God failed."

No, you're not trusting the outcome. You need to be trusting in God's character. Did you get that? You are not to trust for the outcome. You are to trust in the nature and character of God.

So, what that means is, whatever happens, as I wait for God, trusting in Him, I am remembering His goodness, His character and His faithfulness. And if, in that waiting, the answer becomes no, I trust Him. I trust Him because He is God. And so, my expectation is in His promises, and His character, that He is working all things together for good, for those that love Him and are called according to His purpose.

So, as you wait in expectation for God to work all things together for good, for those that love Him and are called according to His purpose, and if that's you today, do not worry about what is in front of you. God is going to work all things together for good. All things. Not some things. Not a handful of things. All things together for good because He loves you and, if you are called according to His purpose, He will move in your life in a way that you would never expect. He will supersede your expectations, but He is asking you to wait and trust.

Do not worry if things are not moving fast enough. They will move just when they are supposed to. God is never late. Sometimes we think He is, but He's never late. He is always right on time.

Lets Pray: Father, thank You for those that are reading today. I thank You for Your hand over their lives. I pray that You would give them the courage and strength to wait and trust You, to expect from no one God, but You, Your goodness, Your mercy, and Your faithfulness. May they trust that You are at work in their life Lord God. Let us not resent the word 'wait.' But instead, let us recognize it as Your fashioning tool used to teach us to trust You more. We will give You all the circumstances in our life, Lord God. We surrender them to You and wait silently for You alone. We love You, Jesus. Amen.

Freedom Starts with Agreement!

"Stand therefore in the freedom
which Christ has purchased for you,
and do not once again be ensnared with bondage."
Galatians 5:1 NIV

I want us to look at Galatians 5:1 together. It says, "Stand therefore in the freedom which Christ has purchased for you, and do not once again be ensnared with bondage." As I preach in different places, I get to see God on display. I get to see the demon possessed delivered. I get to see Christ set people in bondage free. I get to see people physically healed in front of my eyes. I get to see people touched by the power of God like you couldn't imagine. These people are never the same again.

Christ came to set us free. That's what He came to do. We don't have to wait until heaven to be free. Freedom is here now on earth. He came that we would be free, and the scripture adds a little exclamation point, "free indeed" (John 8:36). He's called us and commissioned us to walk in freedom. We don't have to be in bondage to unforgiveness, fear, anxiety, or anything else!
We don't have to be in bondage to our past or to the things that have hurt us. We don't have to be in bondage to wrong thought patterns or unhealthy thought patterns. We can walk in liberty. Christ has won you liberty, but you have to stay in liberty. You can be set free and the Bible says, "then become entangled again to bondage, to the yoke of bondage." And you ask, "Well, how do I do that?" Being entangled again happens really simply. All I have to do is begin to come in agreement with things that are

against the word of God.

Satan brings the thought that is contrary to the word of God. When I begin to walk in agreement with the lies that Satan has strategically planted, I now have opened myself up again to be entangled, to be trapped in bondage yet again. The word of God brings us freedom. The word of God brings us liberty. The spirit of the Lord brings us freedom, "where the spirit of the Lord is there is freedom" (2 Corinthians 3:17). There is freedom from things that are in our past, our hurts, our insecurities, our fears, our anxieties, our brokenness and our abuses. All those things are set free by the spirit of God and by the word of God.

But if I walk in agreement with Satan and his lies and not in agreement with God and His word, then I've opened myself up again for the yoke of bondage. And the Lord is saying, "Be careful. I've set you free."

Today, I want to challenge you. If you're not free, it's okay. Identify it and get around people that can pray you free. Get around people that can help you walk in freedom. Say, "I have this issue with unforgiveness," "I have this issue with my past and I don't want to carry it anymore," or "I have this issue with this or that." Or whatever it is.

Allow people to pray for you. If you don't have a group of people that can pray with you, then email me and I'll pray with you. My desire is to see the body of Christ free, so email me at MarshaMansour.com and I'll gladly pray with you and believe God for your freedom. But, once He has set you free, child of God, understand that you need to decide to walk in freedom every day.

Say, "I am not going to align myself with the enemy. If the enemy speaks, it will always be something contrary to what the word of God speaks and I'm not going to agree with it. I'm going to rebuke it and stand on the word." That's how we stay out of bondage. But, if we continue to agree with what the enemy says, then we've welcomed bondage back into our life.

And the heart of Jesus, child of God, is that you would walk free. That nothing will hold you, nothing would bind you, and that you would walk in liberty. So my heart for you is that you would choose liberty. Don't buy the lies, don't agree with them. When the enemy comes and tells you lies, don't say, "Well, that's true," and walk with it because the second you do that you've opened yourself up for bondage. When the enemy speaks, know that he's a liar and that he's the father of lies. Don't accept what he says. Accept what the word says about you, your circumstances, your future, your family, and accept only what the word says! Accept what the spirit of the Lord says, and only Him.

Walk in liberty, child of God.

Father, I pray for Your children. I thank You that You have made us free and "free indeed," God. Your word is clear, that we're to stand firm in the freedom that You have given us. And Lord, we ask God that You would help us and make us wise and discerning, not to become entangled again with the yoke of bondage, but that we would walk in freedom at all times, God, because You've called us to be free. And so, Father, we receive freedom. We receive freedom in every area.

Lets Pray: Father, I pray for those that are not free. Those that know in their heart that there's unforgiveness, yokes from the past or yokes of fear, anxiety, or other forms of bondage binding them today. Father, I declare freedom over them in the name of Jesus. That You will touch them even as we pray right now. Father, I pray that You would put people around them to help them walk and live in freedom. I pray that You would cause Your children to live free and "free indeed." And that freedom would be theirs every day. Amen!

Run to the Rock

"When I am overwhelmed,
lead me to the rock that is higher than I."
Psalms 61:2 NKJV

Greetings!

The book of Psalms is loaded with simple sentences that are filled with great wisdom! Verses like Psalms 61:2. It's a short verse, but it's filled with wisdom. It says, "When I am overwhelmed, lead me to the rock that is higher than I." It is very easy for us to become overwhelmed. Life is overwhelming. Many times when we wake up in the morning, we're already on the "go." We already have our to-do list ready and prepared before we even get out of bed –"Got to get this done and that done." If anything throws it off course, we become overwhelmed because that's our human nature.

The Lord is saying, "When you become overwhelmed, come to Me. Be led to the rock that's higher than you." The reason the scripture gives the illustration of a rock is because it's something that is secure, something that's solid. Lead me to the rock that's high. Me and you are not secure. We're not rocks. We're sand. We're not stable. We're not secure. We're not wise. We're wise in our own eyes. We're not wise in the things that we need to be wise in and we become overwhelmed easily.

Life overwhelms. There are things that come in life that are incredibly overwhelming (i.e. sickness, ailments, issues at work, issues at home, divorce, etc.). We watch people struggle with depression, discouragement, and fear. Those things are overwhelming. The scripture says "when you are overwhelmed," not "if you are overwhelmed." There are moments that all of us are going to be overwhelmed.

When you are overwhelmed, your prayer should be, "Lord, lead me to the rock that's higher than I. Lead me to that sure ground. Let me run to You and be on that sure ground that's higher than me." You don't want something at your level when you're overwhelmed. You want something bigger, you want something higher, you want something stronger, you want something more secure because you can't do it in your own strength. You can't take care of it on your own because you are not able to handle it. You are not enough. You need something much bigger.

Pray that God would lead you to the rock that is higher than you. Ask him to secure you. Ask him to strengthen you. Ask him to wrap His arms around you, and to not only lead you to that rock, but strengthen you to stay at that rock. And as you stay at that rock, you will watch as that rock meets the things that overwhelm you and watch them disintegrate because your rock is a sure foundation.

God is a sure foundation. You don't have to worry, He's got you.

But, the only way the things around you can overwhelm you and keep overwhelming you is if you don't go to Him. If you continue to operate on your own, you will be overwhelmed all the time. But, if you are led to the rock that is higher than you, it will protect you, it will guard you, it will cover you, it will secure you, and you'll be able to walk in everything God has for you.

Lets Pray: Father, I pray for those reading today. I pray that You bless them. I pray that You encourage them. I pray that You anoint them. God, I pray that You would lead them to the rock that is higher than them and that You would draw them in close and strong. Lord God, I pray, for anyone who feels overwhelmed today, that You would just cover them with Your grace and Your mercy and that You would have Your hand over them, Lord God. I pray, Lord God, that You would encourage them and that they would always remember that You are a solid foundation and that You're with them and for them. God bless them. I pray in Jesus name. Amen.

The Blueprint to Victory

"Submit yourself to the Lord. Resist the devil and he will flee. Draw near unto God, and He will draw near unto you."
James 4:7 NIV

I want to share out of the book of James. James 4:7 says, "Submit yourself to the Lord. Resist the devil and he will flee. Draw near unto God, and He will draw near unto you." I want to take a minute to break that down. I love that God's word is so incredibly practical and so incredibly clear. In the book of James, it gives us these clear steps on how to walk after God in a certain way.

You know, oftentimes, I hear people say, "I struggle with things that the enemy is constantly attacking me with," "I struggle in my flesh with temptation," and "I struggle in my flesh with these other things." In James, the scripture is saying something very clear. It doesn't say "resist the devil first," it says "submit yourself to the Lord" first.

What does "submit yourself to the Lord" mean?

It means to submit yourself to the word of God. Submit yourself to the person of God. Put yourself under the word of God. Yield to it. Don't try and have your way, but instead have His way. When you fully submit yourself to God, it means that you put yourself under the word of God and then you are able to resist the devil. See, if you don't submit yourself under the word of God, you don't have a leg to stand on against the devil. You can't fight him. The way to fight the enemy is to submit yourself under the word of God.

There's a story in scripture where Paul is praying for demon possessed people. As he prays for them. they're delivered. As Paul prays for the people, seven brothers, called "the seven brothers of Sceva," see him praying over the demon possessed. So, they decide that they're going to do the same thing.

They find a person that's demon possessed and they say to him, "We rebuke you in the name of Jesus, that Paul believes." They don't know Jesus. They say, "We rebuke you in the name of Jesus, who Paul believes." And you know what happens to those seven brothers? The demon turns around and says, "Paul I know. Jesus I know. You, I don't know." The demon then proceeds to beat up the seven brothers.

These brothers were trying to resist the devil so that he would flee from them, but they weren't submitting to God. It doesn't work that way. There are orders to what God does .God says first, 'Put yourself under Me, submit to Me. Then resist the devil.' Now, you have a leg to stand on.

Resist the devil and he's going to flee from you. You don't have to flee from the enemy, he will flee from you. You don't have to fight these temptations on your own and try to figure out. Put opposition to him and he will flee.

Here is the key: Draw near to God and He promises that as you draw near, He will draw near to you.

I don't know who's reading this today, but I just feel in my heart that some of you who are reading feel very far from God. God is saying, "I haven't moved. I'm right where you left me. Just draw near. Come close to Me. Say My name." Sometimes, we don't realize that drawing near to God is as simple as saying the name of Jesus. You close your eyes and say, "Jesus." As you do that, He just increases and you begin to draw near.

Praying without ceasing doesn't mean that I'm stopping my entire day and just praying. It means that I'm in a conscious state of understanding my need for God.

So when you're drawing near to God, you just begin to say His name all day. "Jesus, I need you. Jesus, I need you." That's drawing near to God. "God, I can't do this without You. I'm in need of You God. Please draw close to me." The Bible says that as you draw close, He will draw close. He hasn't moved. As you put out your hand, He will put out His and take hold of yours, and He'll walk with you. You do not have to feel far from God.

You don't have to feel defeated by the enemy. There is a blueprint that God has given us in the book of James on how to resist the enemy. It says, "Submit yourself to God." Submit your will, your character, your desires, your dreams, and your ambitions. Submit it all to God. Resist the enemy and he'll run from you. Then, continue to draw near to Him and, as you do that, He will draw near to you. You don't have to feel far from God today. He is as close as the mention of His name.

Lets Pray: God, I pray for Your people, that You'd give them the ability and the courage to submit themselves to You. Submit themselves to Your word, to resist the enemy, and watch the enemy flee from in front of them. Lord God, give them the courage to draw near to You. Anyone that feels far today, God, stir their heart so that they don't have to stay there. They can just begin to reach for You, and You will reach right back to them, Lord God. I pray that You bless them, that You anoint them, that You walk with them, Lord God. Have Your way we pray, in all of their lives, in Jesus name. Amen.

Recklessly Obey

"The Lord spoke to Abraham and said, 'Go from your country, go from your family, leave your father's house and go to the land that I will show you'"
Genesis 12:1 NKJV

In 2019, I stepped away from 28 years of pastoring in the local church to being a pastor to the Church at large. The first day I attended a church not as one of the pastors was a very nostalgic and a very surreal day. But, God was so good and so faithful and His voice was so clear! In the midst of that, He spoke to me though in Genesis 12:1. Genesis 12:1 says, "The Lord spoke to Abraham and said, 'Go from your country, go from your family, leave your father's house and go to the land that I will show you.'" I want to tell you, if you look at that and you say, "That's an incomplete statement," it actually isn't. It's a very complete statement.

God is speaking to Abraham and He says, "Go from your country, go from your family, go from your father's house to a land that I will show you." I want to tell you none of those pronouns are a mistake. God is making a very clear point to Abraham. It goes on a little further in the verse and God says, "When you do that, I'm going to make you a father of great nations. I'm going to bless you. I'm going to bless everyone that blesses you and curse everyone that curses you, and I will walk with you and I will give you all that you need." There is a key in this verse that God is speaking about. It's the key that I also walk in and I pray that you are also getting excited about walking in these new truths.

The key is that, as long as we're comfortable in our country, with our family and in our father's house, we will never go to the land that God has for us because comfort and security are the things that hold us back from the more that God has for us. God says to Abraham, "I want you to leave all these things that are secure: your country, your family, and your father's house. And go." There's another version of the scripture that says, "To a land that you don't know, but I'm going to show you."

What God is saying to Abraham is, "Will you obey me? Will you go to a land that you don't know, a land that I'm going to show you, and walk after what I have for you?" As Abraham does that, God says, "As you do that, I will bless you. I'll be with you. I'll walk with you." He's giving Abraham a promise, but it's a conditional promise. It's not one of these promises that, boom, automatically happened.

God said, "Abraham, you're going to be the father of a great nation." Following this He says, "There's a condition to that. For you to walk in the blessing that I have for you, you're going to have to step into some faith, you're going to have to step into some trust. You're going to have to leave the things that are familiar and comfortable and easy to step into what I have for you."

I want to tell you something, child of God. Maybe this is not what God is asking you to do. That's okay. You don't have to take these kinds of steps, but maybe God is asking you to take a different kind of step. Maybe He's asking you to be uncomfortable at work, or uncomfortable in different places of your life, or in your family about sharing His word, or praying for people, or for stepping out of what's comfortable. See, comfort will always be the thief of what God wants to do in your life. It always will because the things of God are going to make you uncomfortable. The things of the supernatural are going to make you uncomfortable, and so you have to make a decision in your heart that those things are not going to rob you of the things God has for you.

I'm willing to be uncomfortable and recklessly obey God because I know God has a plan for me. I want to challenge and encourage you. Step into the uncomfortability of walking in obedience. It's okay to be uncomfortable. It's okay to not always know or feel like I'm in my house, my country, or with my family. It's okay to rest in the arms of the Lord and say, "God, I trust You. I don't know what You're doing. You're taking me to a land that I don't know, but that's okay. I just trust You."

So, today, I want to encourage you and remind you that you serve a good God and that you don't have to know everything. As a matter of fact, you don't have to know anything. You just have to know what He says, and take that step into what He has for you. As you do this, I promise you, God will bless you tremendously.

Since I recklessly obeyed God and left my full time pastoral job, I don't have enough time to tell you all the testimonies that have happened. I don't have enough time to tell you all that God has done. I am riding on the wings and the wave of faith. I am so excited for what God is doing and I want you to be excited about what God wants to do in your life. But understand that it's on the thresholds of what you're afraid of leaving.

I heard Craig Groeschel (senior pastor of the biggest church in America) say, "Our greatest point of victory is right on the brink of our greatest fear." That's the truth. When you lose your security and comfort and look fear in the face and say, "I refuse to let you rob me," and walk over to what God has for you, man, on the other side is breakthrough, healing, deliverance and abundant blessing.

So, I encourage you, go with God. Leave your country. Leave your family. Leave your father's house and go to an unfamiliar land that God is leading you to. He never leads us in the wrong way.

Lets Pray: Lord, I pray that You place Your hand upon Your children. That You'd lead them and that You'd give them the courage to be obedient. Recklessly obedient, God. I pray, God, that You would cover them with Your blood and with Your grace and that the sound of Your voice will be sufficient for them to move, Lord God. I ask You to give them a heart to obey. Draw them so close to You, in Jesus' name. Amen.

How to Obtain Peace

"He will keep him in perfect peace whose mind is stayed on Him because he has trusted in Him."
Isaiah 26:3 NKJV

What a great God we serve! He loves us so much and longs to see us walking and living in all that He has for us! One of the things that He wants us to walk in is peace! It's clear in Isaiah 26:3 which says, "He will keep him in perfect peace whose mind is stayed on Him because he has trusted in Him." I want to talk to you about this word "peace" because I think, oftentimes, we get confused.

We think peace is the byproduct of our circumstances or situations, and that's not true. You can be in the worst situation and have peace, because it's not a byproduct of what you're walking through. Peace is a byproduct of your relationship with the Lord and a byproduct of trusting the Lord. That's why the verse says He will keep him in perfect peace whose mind is stayed on Him because he's trusted in Him. See, peace is a byproduct of trusting and relying on the Lord Jesus Christ.

If you think peace comes in your circumstances, I'm going to tell you, child of God, you will never have peace because your circumstance will never indicate peace. They will never bring you peace. But the scripture is clear that God himself will keep you in perfect peace because your mind is stayed on Him. When our minds are on the things of God, on the promises of God, and on the character of God, peace is the byproduct of that.

So, child of God, I want to challenge you to get your mind on the things of God. I don't know what you're walking through. I don't know what's going on in your life. I don't know what circumstances are before you, but I want to tell you that it doesn't matter what it is. It matters that God is for you and that God is with you and because of that you can have peace in the worst circumstances.

There are people that walk through atrocities and they have peace. You know why? Because their minds are steadfast on the Lord, so God sustains them and, then, they have perfect peace. They're not walking around fragmented or lost or confused. God holds them up and they can look and respond in a way that is godly because peace is on them, and because their minds are on the Lord.

See, when you remember the character of God, when you remember the word of God, He's able to sustain you. He's able to hold you. Perfect peace becomes how you walk and how you live. If you feel an unrest in your spirit, if you feel overwhelmed by what you're walking through, if you feel discouraged and defeated, I want to ask you, where is your mind? What are you thinking about? Who are you allowing to have top place in your thoughts? Because if it is anything else besides the Lord, you won't have perfect peace. But, if your mind is steadfast on the Lord, you'll have perfect peace regardless of what you're walking through. The scripture says because you've "trusted in Him," He will sustain you. God wants His people to walk in peace regardless of what's going on.

So I'm going to challenge you to put your mind on Him steadfast. What does that mean? It means not moving; staying consistent on the Lord and as a result, peace will be the byproduct. Learn to be steadfast in the Lord. Learn to trust Him in every circumstance, regardless of what you see and what you feel. I promise you, you will be covered with God's perfect peace.

Lets Pray: Lord Jesus, touch Your people. I pray that if their mind is on anything but You, Your character and Your word, that You would challenge them, that You would bring their heart in alignment with Your word and with Your promises and with Your character. Father, I pray that You cover them with Your perfect peace. That You would sustain them as they trust You. That peace would cover them. That You would guide them and that Your peace would lead them every morning. Strengthen them and encourage them. In the name of Jesus we pray! Amen!

May You Prosper

"Beloved, I pray that you may prosper in all things and be in health, just as your soul prospers."
3 John 1:2 NKJV

"**D**o you know the Lord wants His people to prosper! "May you prosper in all things and be in health, just as your soul prospers." (3 John 1:2). The Lord's heart is that we would prosper in all things and that there would be no area in our life that was lacking. God's desire is that you would prosper.

Now the word prosper in many Christian circles has a negative connotation. We think of the prosperity teachers that talk about pink Cadillacs and multimillion-dollar mansions.It's great if God wants to bless you, but that's not what the Scripture is talking about. It's talking about prospering; that you are blessed. That you are blessed in every area of your life and are doing well. It means your relationships, finances, job, schooling are prospering. Scripture also adds "even your health."

Child of God, our God is a God that heals. He is a God that has given us divine health. It is His good pleasure that His children would be healthy. If you're struggling with sickness today whether it is diabetes, rheumatoid arthritis, cancer, or something else, it is the will of God that you would prosper, that you would be healed. Healing belongs to the household of faith. It is part of our inheritance. The Bible calls it the bread of the children. The Word also says "By his stripes, we are healed and made whole." Jesus has purchased healing for us.

John is saying, "I pray that He prospers you in all ways," and then he goes a little further, "Even in your health, that you would be healthy. You would be whole" - in mind, body, and soul. Your thoughts, your mental state would be healthy. You wouldn't be filled with fear, rejection, depression, or anxiety. Your mind would be healthy. You would be filled in your spirit with the things of God.

Scripture says that your strength would match your days. As long as God gives you life, He'll give you strength for that life. You would prosper in everything; in your finances, in your job, in your relationships. If there is a lack in those areas, begin to declare the Word over these things. Begin to stand in faith, and say, "Lord, I want my relationships to prosper. I want my health to prosper. I want my finances to prosper. God, I want all these things prospering, because my soul is prospering."

What it means is, as I'm connected to God, and my soul is prospering, I'm growing in the things of God. The byproduct of my soul prospering is that everything in my life would begin to prosper. Now that doesn't mean that if struggles come you and God are not okay. No, it just means the enemy is attacking.

There are things that are just part of nature that we're fighting against in this world. Even though we live in a fallen world, it's God's heart that you would prosper in all things. Child of God, begin to ask God to cause you to prosper. As your soul prospers and as you grow closer to the Lord, may the fruit of your life be that everything about you prospers.

Lets Pray: Father, I pray, for Your children. I pray, God, that they would prosper in all things: their health, their finances, their relationships, their mental status, their emotions, Lord God, their jobs, their schooling, everything about them. God, as their soul prospers, as they draw close to You, may the byproduct of that relationship be that everything around them prospers and may their strength match their days. I pray for any one that's sick in their body today. I declare healing over them in the Name of

Jesus. I command every sickness, every infirmity to bow its knee at the Name of Jesus, and I thank You that by Your stripes, we are healed and made whole. Touch them with divine healing. In Jesus' Name. Amen

Wait for the Vision

Then the Lord answered me and said, 'Write the vision and make it plain on tablets that he may run who reads it. For the vision is yet for an appointed time; but at the end it will speak. It will not lie. Though it tarries, wait for it; because it will surely come, it will not tarry'"
Habakkuk 2:2, 3 NKJVP

The Bible is filled with many recordings of visions. God uses visions to speak His purposes. In Habakkuk 2:2-3 God does just that. It says, "Then the Lord answered me and said, 'Write the vision and make it plain on tablets that he may run who reads it. For the vision is yet for an appointed time. But at the end it will speak. It will not lie. Though it tarries, wait for it; because it will surely come it will not tarry.'" In this verse, God is encouraging someone because their heart is discouraged. They're not seeing what they think they should be seeing. They're thinking, "God I have this vision. I have this idea. I thought You spoke, God, but it's not coming to pass." And the Lord says, 'Write it down. Write it down. Write it plain; write it clear so he who reads it will run.'

So as we read it, we run.

Even though it seems like it's not moving, it will speak. It will not lie. It will speak. It will not lie. Though it tarry, wait for it. For it will truly come to pass. The word 'tarry' is a word that we used to use in church. We don't seem to use it now, but it's a very important word. Though it tarries, though it delays, it will surely come to pass. We lose hope in delay because we forget. We lose hope because we think delay means denial. We think delay means something is not going to happen.

Delay is simply that; it's delayed. It doesn't have another meaning. It doesn't mean, "Oh, it's delayed so God's not going to do it." It literally means that it's delayed. But, the Scripture here is clear. It will come to pass.

So, child of God, I want to encourage you. There are visions, there are dreams, there are hopes, there are things that you so deeply sense in your heart and it looks like they're not coming to pass. The Lord is saying, "Listen. The vision is there. Write it down."

Do you know why He wants you to write it down? He wants to make it clear. Make it plain. I'm not playing games. Write it down. Put it down on paper. This is the vision that I've given you. This is the purpose that I've given. This is the word I've given you. Write it down. Make it plain so he who reads it will run.

As we read it, we get inspired. We get encouraged. We get ignited saying, "God said it. God said it so I'm going to run with this." So he who reads it runs. It goes on to say, "For the vision is yet for an appointed time." It's for an appointed time; it's not for every season. We get confused with that. We're asking, "God, where's the promise?" God's saying, "It's for an appointed time. It's for a very specific moment."

We look at the story of Lazarus. Jesus knew that Lazarus would die if He didn't show up and yet He waited until after Lazarus died before He showed up. He didn't show up the first day. He showed up on the fourth day. There was a reason He came on the fourth day. In those days, the people believed the spirit of man dwelled in people for three days after they died. Jesus was making a very clear point by coming on the fourth day. Nobody else understood that but Jesus. On the fourth day, He resurrected Lazarus. Nobody could say it was anything more than His authority and His power. Lazarus' resurrection was for an appointed time.

The vision that God has given you is for an appointed time. Though it tarry, it will speak. It will happen. It will not lie. Though it tarry, wait for it. It will surely come to pass. God does not lie. His word does not lie. Though something seems delayed it does not mean denial. It just means God is setting up the appointed time to meet you and to do exactly what He said.

He is faithful to His word. Don't worry. Just write it down. Run for it. Believe God. Know it's an appointed time. Don't get lost in the delay. Don't get discouraged by the delay. Keep moving, keep trusting, keep believing, and keep writing. Write it down and keep believing that even in the delay, God is in it because in the delay something is happening that you and I do not understand.

As it tarries, we wait, for it will surely come to pass. The word 'surely' appears in that chapter three times. Surely; that's God's exclamation point. He's going to do it. So trust Him today as you reflect, as you plan and as you dream. Just begin to let that permeate into your heart and in your spirit. For surely God keeps His word. He doesn't lie.

Delay never means denial. It just means delay. There's always purpose in the delay. May God's vision in His heart permeate in your heart.

Lets Pray: Father, I pray that this word would speak to Your children. It would encourage them and it would ignite them, Lord. That You are in the delay and that You are faithful, God. You don't lie. Your word will speak and the vision You have given each one of us will speak. It's for an appointed time for our best and for Your glory. Amen!

Delight in the Lord

"Delight yourself in the Lord
and He will give you the desires of your heart."
Psalms 37:4 NKJV

I am so honored to just speak God's word into you. When preaching and ministering the word of God, I get to see God move with such great power and I always walk away feeling refreshed and blessed. People always ask "when you minister, do you get tired?" The truth is I really don't. I might get physically tired, but my spirit is so strong because I get to see God moving in His power and truth. When ministering, I also get to see His heart, which is to have his people walk in everything He has for them.

That's the reason I get so excited with these devotionals. With every page, I am believing for God to show up and touch you with the transformational power of His word! Our word today speaks of transformation. Psalms 37:4 says, "Delight yourself in the Lord and He will give you the desires of your heart." This verse is married to Matthew 6:33, where it says, "Seek first the Kingdom of God and His righteousness and all these things will be added onto you." They're very similar in their understanding and the Bible says here, "Delight yourself in the Lord and He will give you the desires of heart." We have all these deep desires in our hearts, these things that we so long for, these things that we want, and the Bible says don't put your focus there. Don't put your efforts there. There are things that we simply cannot make happen. They're desires, but we can't make them happen. The Lord is saying, "Don't focus there. Be with Me. Delight in Me. Find your pleasure in Me."

The story of Ruth talks about a woman who was just delighting herself before the Lord and gleaning and doing the things of God. As she's doing that, God lines her right up to being in the eye shot of Boaz, and when she's there, He gives her everything that she wanted. The Lord is saying to us today, "Don't worry about these things that you want, these things that you're longing for. Just be present with Me. Put My kingdom first." It doesn't even say to make it a routine. He says delight in it.

Delight in the things of the Lord. Delight in being with the Lord. Delight in the Lord and He, in turn, will give you the desires of your heart. Let me tell you something about that. When you delight in the Lord, if you have desires that are ungodly desires, if you have desires that God does not have for you, as you delight in Him, He'll shift your desires. He will cause your desires and the things that you want to line up with what He wants, because He knows what's best anyway. We think we know what's best, but the truth is we don't know a thing. We need Him to lead us. We need Him to guide us. We need Him to instruct us because God knows the end to this story; we don't. We just know what we want today and, oftentimes, some of that is wrong.

So the Bible says "delight yourself in the Lord," and be in His presence. What does that mean, "be in His presence?" What is it like to delight yourself in someone's presence? Be with Him, talk with Him, share with Him, be vulnerable with Him, laugh with Him, do life with God every day.

Delight yourself in Him and He, in turn, will give you the desires of your heart. He'll give back to you the things that you're craving and that you want. He will bless you with them and, if they're not what you need, He'll change them to match His, to do what is best for you. Ultimately, what He's doing is working for your best, for your benefit and for His glory all in the same moment. Your best and His glory are happening at the same moment when we delight ourselves in the Lord.

I'm going to encourage you, don't seek a million different things. Don't be a seeker of things. Be a seeker of God. Don't look for His hands, look for His heart! Spend time with God hear Him, press into Him, be close to Him, talk to Him. Maybe some of you've never prayed like that before. That's okay. Talk to God the way you would talk to anybody. Just begin to open up your mouth to Him.

If you don't know how to talk to him, open up the word of God. It will help you know how to talk to God. It'll help you know how to direct your prayer appropriately and effectively. As you do that, the desires of your heart will be fulfilled in front of you.

Lets Pray: Jehovah, I pray for Your children, that You would teach them how to delight in You, Lord God. Teach them how to be in Your presence, how to enjoy Your company and how to allow Your presence to change and to shift them. Father, as they delight in You, I thank You that Your word is clear and that You, in turn, will give them the desires of their heart. Lord God, I pray that You bless them and that You use them. Have Your way over them. I pray in Jesus name. Make Yourself so real to them in Jesus name. Amen.

Draw Near to Him

"Draw near to God and He will draw near to you."
James 4:8 NKJV

Praying that you are refreshed and blessed as you read this today! As we look into our Scripture, I am praying for someone to be encouraged today. James 4:8 says, "Draw near to God and He will draw near to you." I know there are plenty of seasons we walk through where we feel like God is not near. He seems far, as though we are walking through stuff and He's just not near me. I can't sense Him. I can't feel Him.

The Bible is clear that He will never leave us or forsake us. He hasn't moved, child of God. He's exactly where He said He would be. So if you don't feel near to God, I challenge you that the person who moved is you. God is close. He is near to you. He is right beside you. But, something has caused the distance.

What has allowed you to feel this way? Is it that you've been careless with your walk with Him? Are you being lazy about seeking Him? Are you listening to other voices and other influences? Are other things going on around you? Are other things taking your attention and your affection? Any of these things can make you feel distant from God.

James makes it really easy to solve! He says, "Draw near." Begin to get close. Begin to draw near to Him. Begin to seek Him and spend time with Him, and begin to look for Him. Begin to close your ears to the things that are not of Him. Begin to connect your heart with the things that are of Him. Begin to bring worship around you. Put worship music on and begin to just draw near to

Him.

The Scripture says that as you draw near, He instantly will draw near. There are seasons that we walk through that drawing near seems like a lot of effort because we're tired and we're frustrated and we are discouraged. In those moments, drawing near is just simply saying His Name.

It is as simple as that - just say "Jesus." I promise you that in those moments as you close your eyes and you just say the Name of Jesus, His love and His grace will overwhelm you. He will draw near to you, because the Bible says that He inclines His ear to the voice of His children. As you speak, child of God, (remember you're His child) His heart is overwhelmed at your voice – that's how much He loves you. When you say His Name, the Bible says He inclines His ear to you. That is how He draws near to you.

I don't know what you're walking through today. It doesn't matter. All I know is that God is near to you. If you feel far from Him, just begin to call out His Name. If you want to feel closer to Him, just begin to call Him. Just begin to focus your eyes and your heart upon Him. That is what drawing near means. As you begin to focus your eyes, your heart, your affection on him, He will be ever near.

Lets Pray: Jehovah, I pray for Your children, that You would teach them how to delight in You, Lord God. Teach them how to be in Your presence, how to enjoy Your company and how to allow Your presence to change and to shift them. Father, as they delight in You, I thank You that Your word is clear and that You in turn will give them the desires of their heart. Lord God, I pray that You bless them and that You use them. Have Your way over them I pray in Jesus name. Make Yourself so real to them in Jesus name. Amen.

It is Time to Get Lite

"Therefore we also, since we are surrounded by so great a cloud of witnesses, let us lay aside every weight, and the sin which so easily ensnares us, and let us run with endurance the race that is set before us."
Hebrews 12:1 NKJV

Our verse today is found in Hebrews 12:1. It says, "Therefore we also, since we are surrounded by so great a cloud of witnesses, let us lay aside every weight, and the sin which so easily ensnares us, and let us run with endurance the race that is set before us." When the Bible speaks of the cloud of witnesses, it is speaking about all those that have gone ahead of us; all those that have laid a path. People found in Scripture, like Moses and Abraham, David and Deborah, Abigail, Paul and Peter. Those are some of those great men and women who have gone before. Since we're surrounded by such a great cloud of witnesses, people who have blazed the trail, and in spite of their flaws, have shown us the way, then let us lay aside every weight and the sin that so easily entangles or ensnares us.

The Bible makes a distinction between weight and sin. There are things that are obviously sin. You need to lay those aside. You are called to live a blameless holy life. You need to be diligent to release yourself of sin and say, "That's not how I'm going to live anymore." Then, there's this other word 'weight.' Weight are those things that are not beneficial to us. They actually weigh us down.

When runners are getting ready for a race, you don't see them putting on heavy clothes. Instead, you see them putting on light clothes. They get rid of all the excess weight because they want to be able to run light. Their shoes and clothing have to be a certain size and a certain weight. Why? They want to be fast.

You, child of God, need to get rid of things that are weighing you down, things that are not of God, things that are not beneficial. They may not be sin, but they don't benefit you. Maybe it's how you spend your time, or the people that are around you, or some of the choices you make. They're not sinful but they're not beneficial.

The Scripture tells us to lay aside those weights and sin that so easily entangle us. When these things are part of our life, they easily entangle us. "And let us run with perseverance the race that is set before us." God is saying, "If You, child of God, want to run this race properly, you will have to get real lite. You have to get rid of everything that weighs you down. You've got to get light on your feet so you can run the race with endurance."

This isn't a sprint. We haven't been called to run a sprint. We've been called to run a marathon, and that marathon requires endurance. It requires, steady, steady running. To be able to do that, you need to get lite. You could have a little extra weight if you're running a sprint, but if you're running a marathon, you need to have endurance. God is saying, "Let's get some endurance in my people. Get rid of the sin. Get rid of the weight."

You have people that have gone before you that have already done it. They've laid a path for you. Look at their example and live by their example. Run this race with endurance." God has a great race for you. He has a great plan for you. You want to be in the best position to receive everything He has for you.

Lets Pray: Father, I pray for those reading today, give them courage and strength to lay aside every weight and every sin that so easily entraps them. I pray, God, you fill each one of us with endurance to run the race that is set before us for, Your glory. We thank You for all who have gone before us. May we learn from their example Father. And may we be the people that You've called us to be. In Jesus' Name. Amen.

He Fights Our Battles

"Be strong and courageous, do not fear or be dismayed because of the king of Assyria, nor because of all the army that is with him; for the One with us is greater than the one with him. With him there is only an arm of flesh, but with us is the Lord our God to help us and to fight our battles."
2 Chronicles 32:7-8 AMP

There is a real enemy that has been fighting the people of God from the beginning. But, amazingly, we never have to battle alone! In 2 Chronicles 32, starting at verse 7, God shows us a battle plan. "Be strong and courageous. Do not fear or be dismayed because the king of Assyria, nor because of all the army that is with him; for the One with us is greater than the one with him. With him there is only an arm of flesh, but with us is the Lord our God to help us and to fight our battles." Israel was fighting the King of Assyria and Israel was surrounded. There was no way out. They were outnumbered on every side. King Hezekiah began to encourage his troops. "Don't worry about the kingdoms here. Don't be afraid. Don't be dismayed. Don't fear the King of Assyria. Don't be afraid of the multitude that's with him. The One with us is greater than the one with him. He only has the arm of flesh with him. We have Jehovah, who fights our battles."

In the natural, those words sounded ridiculous. They were outnumbered, in both manpower and firepower. They had no way to win in the flesh, in the natural. But Hezekiah saw something different. He was looking with a different eye, and a different focus. Hezekiah understood that is was not about what he could see but rather about the power of God. He believed that God was greater.

Hezekiah wasn't concerned because they were outnumbered. "We might be surrounded. But greater is He that is with us, than they that are coming against us. They just have the arm of flesh. We have the supernatural. We have the King of Kings and the Lord of Lords, and He fights my battles."

There have been times in my life when I truly felt surrounded on every end. However, I found He, that is with me, is greater in number than those coming against me. When I felt surrounded, at the end of the day, all they had was the arm of the flesh but I had the King of Kings and the Lord of Lords, and He declared victory over me every time.

I encourage you that victory belongs to you. Whatever is coming at you is just the arm of flesh. You have the King of Kings, and the Lord of Lords, and He fights your battles. You do not have to fight. You just have to stand. It's a big difference. You don't have to take up the battle because you already have the victory. The Lord asks you to trust Him and to have faith.

He is asking you to say, "I'm not going to be dismayed by what I see, because the Lord tells me, 'Don't be afraid. Don't be dismayed. Don't lose focus because of what I see." Even when you don't know how you are going to overcome a situation and you don't know what to do," the Lord is saying, "No, no, no. Don't be afraid. Don't be dismayed. Don't worry about what's coming at you. Know who stands with you. The arm of flesh can't defeat the King of Kings and the Lord of Lords. He stands with you."

Today, if you feel surrounded or overwhelmed and you believe the battle is too big for you, be reassured that all that's in front of you is the arm of flesh. The King of Kings and the Lord of Lords is standing beside you. He fights your battles.

Lets Pray: Father, we thank you that the battle that comes our way, you have already fought. You have already declared victory. I pray for those Lord God who are in the midst of a battle, that You would give them grace and You would give them peace. I pray You would cause them to look at their situation with a different eye, God and not to look with the eye of the flesh, but with the eye of the Spirit, and realize Who is with me is greater than what is coming at me. And victory belongs to me." Help us today, Lord God, to know that it doesn't matter if we feel surrounded, because we know that You are fighting our battles. All that we're surrounded by is You, Lord God. Surround Your people today with grace and mercy and protection. Cover them with Your Spirit, and let them know, Lord God, that they are victorious. We give You all thanks today in Jesus' Name. Amen.

Never Forsaken

"The Lord is faithful, who will establish you and guard you from the evil one."
2 Thessalonians 3:3 NKJV

I'm so encouraged by today's Word found in 2 Thessalonians 3:3. "The Lord is faithful, who will establish you and guard you from the evil one." I always love to be reminded of the faithfulness of the Lord. Oftentimes, we feel like we're walking through life by ourselves and God only appears sporadically and momentarily as we need Him. But that's not the truth. God is a consistent, steady force in our life. He does not cease being faithful. It doesn't matter what's going on, God stays steady. God stays consistent.

Everything around you is going to move. Everything around you is going to shift. There are going to be things that come in that are good, things that come in that are bad, things that are difficult, and things that are hard. In the end, the one thing you can completely rely on is the character of God.

God is faithful. That means He's full of faith and He doesn't move. The Scripture says He will establish you. He'll make your walking and your stepping steadfast. He will settle you. He'll make you solid in where you are. Not only will He establish you but He's even going to guard you from the evil one.

The enemy cannot have his way over you, your family, or over the things that belong to you. The scepter of the wicked does not rest on the land allotted to the righteous. When God has given you something, He guards you. You are His and you belong to

the Lord.
The Word is clear; the faithfulness of God is where we trust. The faithfulness of God is where we lie. The faithfulness of God is where we stand. He is faithful. Every demon in hell is going to come and attack. Every demon in hell is going to want to challenge you to say, "God, where are you? You're not faithful." While we may never verbally say that, there are moments when we think, "God, I'm not sure you're faithful."

Always push back on that thought because the second you begin to forget that God is faithful, you become susceptible to negative thinking. You become susceptible to thoughts that will damage you. Be clear. Your God is faithful. He will establish you and He will guard you from the evil one. He will hold you in His righteous hands. He is faithful. He does not change. No matter what happens, God is faithful and He's looking for people that believe Him and trust Him.

The Book of Hebrews says that without faith, it is impossible to please God because anyone that comes must believe that He is. He is what? Who He says He is. We have to believe that God is who He says He is. When we believe that, and we stand on His character, God is able to do great things for us.

Today, let your heart be filled with faith. Let your heart be encouraged that your God is faithful. Not for one moment, child of God, have you been forsaken. Not for one moment has God forgotten about you. He is faithful to you. He is at your side. He is in front of you. He is behind you. He is faithful and He is constantly establishing you and guarding you from the evil one.

Lets Pray: Father, I pray for Your children. I pray that You would encourage them and You would strengthen them. I pray that You would remind them of Your faithfulness and Your goodness and You would show up, Lord God, in their life in great and mighty ways. Remind them that not for one moment have they ever been forsaken, Lord God. Cover them, I pray, in Jesus' Name. Amen.

Rejoice! Rejoice!

"Rejoice in the Lord always: and again I say, Rejoice."
Philippians 4:4 NIV

Greetings child of God! Today, we will be reading from the Book of Philippians. Philippians 4:4 says, "Rejoice in the Lord always: and again I say, rejoice." This verse has everything to do with a word we throw around pretty easily. It's the word joy. It says, "Rejoice in the Lord always: and again, I say rejoice." We use this word flippantly, and somehow we get confused. We think that joy and happiness are the same thing. I get happy when I like a meal. I get happy when I see someone I like or love. I get happy when I go to a place I enjoy. I get happy when I get a nice email. Those are temporal, emotional responses because something has come into my atmosphere or into my life that has brought me happiness.

Joy is not like that, because we're not happy all the time. Not everything that comes our way makes us happy. So while we're not happy all the time, the Scripture tells us, "Rejoice in the Lord always." There is a requirement of 'joy always.' "Rejoice in the Lord always, and again, I say rejoice." When God says something twice in Scripture, He's making a statement. He doesn't just say, "Rejoice in the Lord always." He says, "Again, I say rejoice." What He is telling us is that joy really isn't an option for a child of God. Joy is a marker of a child of God. We are to be a joyful people. We are to be a people that choose joy.

How do I choose joy? He tells you, "Rejoice." Rejoice in what? The Lord. "Rejoice in the Lord."

Jesus is the same yesterday, today and forever. Since He is consistent and doesn't change, you can rejoice in Him. You can be confident in who He is. Then you can walk in joy because you know that He's going to be the same. You can trust His character. You can trust His Word. Joy should be the byproduct of trusting in the character of God.

I know who God is, and because of that, I can rejoice always. It doesn't matter what comes or what doesn't come, I trust God. I choose to be joyful.

Joy is a choice. People say, "Well, I just lost my joy." No, you chose not to be joyful. You chose to forget who God was. You forgot that He was on the throne. You forgot that nobody moves Him from His throne. You forgot that every promise in His Word is 'yes' and 'amen.' You have forgotten Him. Once you forget Him, it's very easy not to be joyful. As a matter of fact, it's actually impossible. The only way to maintain our joy is to maintain ourselves in Christ.

The Scripture says, "Rejoice in the Lord always," – without ceasing, without stopping. "Rejoice in the Lord always. And again." He's saying, "I reminding you, if you've forgotten, rejoice in the Lord. Rejoice in the Lord always. And again, I say rejoice." It is a mark of a child of God to be joyful. If you are a person who struggles with that, make a decision today. Say, "I refuse to be downcast. I refuse to be discouraged. I refuse to let joy be taken from me."

The Scripture tells us, "the joy of the Lord is your strength." Once joy is taken from you, strength will also be taken from you. You will feel defeated, deflated and destroyed because you cannot rejoice. On the other hand, when I'm rejoicing, I'm looking right at God, and I'm remembering who He is, and I'm living and walking in that and receiving all that comes from it. So, today, child of God, I challenge you, rejoice in the Lord always. And again, I say rejoice.

Lets Pray: I pray for Your children. God, that You would give them strength. I pray, God, that they would remember today who You are and they would rejoice in You at all times. In every circumstance, they would choose joy. Give them the courage to choose joy all the time, to rejoice in the Lord always and again to choose to rejoice. Bless them. I pray, bless this week, God. Remind them of Your goodness and of Your faithfulness, Lord God. Cover them with your grace. In Jesus' Name. Amen.

Our Good Father

"If you then, being evil, know how to give good gifts to your children, how much more will your heavenly Father give the Holy Spirit to those who ask Him!"
Luke 11:13 NKJV

After salvation, the greatest gift that God gives us is the gift of the Holy Spirit. This idea can be found in Luke 11:13. The book of Luke is one of the gospels. Each gospel addresses a specific audience. For example, Matthew is writing to the Jews and Luke is writing to mankind. Luke was Greek. He was writing across the board to everyone in any audience, to convey a message to all people.

In Luke 11:13, he is saying, "Even you who are evil know how to give good gifts to your children. How much more will your Heavenly Father not give the gift of the Holy Spirit to those who ask?" He's making a comparison. He's speaking to all mankind. He's speaking to all of us. He's saying that as human beings, we are evil and even evil mankind, who is sinful and detached from God, knows how to be good to their children. When your children ask for something, you know how to give it to them. He's saying, "You who are evil know how to give good gifts." How much more will your heavenly, holy, righteous God give His children when they ask? When we ask Him for the gift of the Holy Spirit, when we ask Him to bless us, how much more will He give us?

Again, there is a comparison of how much more He will be good to us, His children!! There's this misunderstanding about God, that we don't know Him or He is foreign. God is not foreign. His character is clear. God is good, and not only is He a good God, but He's a good Father. He knows how to care for His children. He knows how to provide for His children. He knows how to make a way for his children. He knows how to open up doors for them that no one else can open.

He's saying to you, "You who are evil know how to give good gifts. How much more do I give my children when they ask for the Holy Spirit?" Why is He desirous of giving the Holy Spirit? Because the most important thing we can ask for is the Holy Spirit.

Why? The Holy Spirit is our Comforter. He's our Protector. He's our advocate. He's a righteous God. He watches out for us. He provides for us. The Holy Spirit is God incarnate walking among the earth and walking with us. So if we're going to ask for anything, we should ask for the Holy Spirit.

The Holy Spirit possesses everything we need: strength, comfort, anointing, freedom, liberty. Everything is encompassed in the Holy Spirit. Essentially, God is saying, "You who are evil know how to give good gifts, but I am a good God. I know how to give the gift that will give you everything.

I encourage you today to trust the heart and the goodness of your Father, your Heavenly Father. For some of you, the word father isn't a good word. I want you to allow the Holy Spirit to reshape that word for you. Don't judge God or His parenting based on some of the parenting that you've seen in your own personal life. God is not a man. He's not subject to the weaknesses and limitations of men. God is a good Father.

You need to begin to judge God on His own merit and the faithfulness He's already shown you. Reflect on your past, consider some challenges you have faced, or the areas in your life where God has seen you through, and where He has proven to be faithful. I want you to begin to ask your good Father for the gift of the Holy Spirit.

He says, "How much more will I give those to my children when they ask Me for the Holy Spirit?" Ask Him generously to pour out His Spirit over you, to make His Spirit real to you, to have the Holy Spirit speak to you, fill you and lead you. When you walk with the Holy Spirit, you'll lack nothing. He'll provide. He'll give you wisdom. He'll protect you and instruct you. He'll touch you with health, wisdom and relationships. Everything that you need is encompassed in the Holy Spirit.

Today, ask for the gift of the Holy Spirit. Trust your good Father to give you the greatest gift. Oftentimes, when we are walking in our life, we can't necessarily see God's Hand working. I want you to understand that you don't have to see His Hands. You just have to trust His heart, that He is good and He is for you and He is beside you. It doesn't matter what you see or what you don't see.

Today, trust the character of your Father, that He is a good Father who cares deeply for the needs, hurts and longings of His children.

Today, embrace God's character and know who He is and walk with Him because we truly serve a good God and we serve a fantastic Father.

Trust Him today, child of God, to be a good Father on your behalf.

Lets Pray: Father, I pray for Your children. I pray You would bless them, God. I pray that You would anoint them. Lord, if the word father is a bad word to them, if it's a negative word, God, today do a washing and a cleansing and a freeing of that word. I pray You would replace those images and those hurts with Your parenting, with Your love, with Your grace, and with Your strength.

I pray, God, You anoint them and You go before them and You pour out Your spirit over them. We're asking you today for the gift of the Holy Spirit to be poured out on everyone reading this today, God. I pray Your Holy Spirit would be poured out over them, Lord God, in great measure today, God. Give us the gift of Your spirit. Holy Spirit, You are welcome in our life, in our being, to lead, to comfort, to strengthen, to walk with us because truly You are the greatest gift and we receive You. In Jesus' Name. Amen.

Put it in your heart and your mind today, that after salvation, the greatest gift that God gives us is the gift of the Holy Spirit. Bless you.

Finish Strong

"I have fought the good fight, I have finished the race, I have kept the faith."
2 Timothy 4:7 NKJV

God has a lot for us to grab hold of in His word today. It's found in 2 Timothy 4:7. The Bible says, "I have fought the good fight. I have finished the race. I have kept the faith." Why is this important to us today? Oftentimes, when we're running after the things of God, we get weary. We begin to get tired. When you're running this race for a long period of time and you're believing God and trying to move after the things of God, there is this moment where you begin to get really tired and weary in your spirit and in your heart. You're trying to run after the things of God and you are just tired.

No one understood that more than the apostle Paul. He was weary. He was tired. He was shipwrecked. He was stoned. He was chased. He was imprisoned. He was anything else you could think of. Just pick your catastrophe; Paul tasted of it. While Paul understood what it was to be weary, he also understood that he had to finish strong. He knew he had to end the race with the same zeal he had when he began the race. He couldn't end any other way. Imagine if he ran the race and then came to the end of this life, fumbled and dropped the whole thing. That's not the heart of God. The heart of God is that with the same zeal and passion we start with, it's the same zeal and passion we finish the race.

I want to speak to your tired, weary heart today and tell you that His grace is sufficient for you. Do not grow weary in well doing.

Don't grow weary. Don't grow tired in doing the right thing. I understand that it's hard. I know what it means to grow weary.

The Scripture encourages us to not grow weary in well doing. You'll reap a harvest if you don't faint. He is faithful. He will do what He says. In the end, you want to be able to say what the apostle Paul said, "I have fought the good fight. I finished my race. I didn't lose it. I didn't fall out. I didn't try to do it in a sprint, but I ran the marathon that was put before me at a good speed, at a good pace. I fought the good fight. I finished my race. I kept my faith. I didn't lose heart."

Many people have started the race, but their weariness, disappointment or frustration caused them to lose their faith and, ultimately, lose the race. What a tragedy it is to run after the things of God and then towards the finish line, you lose your faith.

Keep your faith. He who promised is faithful.

Keep your faith. Trust Him with all of your heart. Fight the good fight. Run your race.

Keep your faith. God is for you. You want to finish strong, child of God.

You want to run every race that's put before you strong. I promise you, God is for you. You want to be tenacious in your pursuit of the things of God and you want to keep your faith with the same zeal that you started. Let it be the same zeal that carries you every day.

If you feel weary today, if you feel tired, just lift your hands to the King of Kings and the Lord of Lords and say, "Lord, I'm weary. I'm tired." Let Him refresh your heart. Get into the word; get into worship. Get around people that know how to pray. Don't allow your weariness to sell your soul and cause you to lose your faith. Finish with your faith intact. Run the race. Fight the fight!

Lets Pray: Father, I pray for every weary heart. I speak a tenacious spirit over them in the name of Jesus. I speak a tenacious heart over them, Father, in the name of Jesus, that they will not allow weariness and fatigue to rob them of what You have for them. Cause them to run the race. Cause them to fight the good fight. Cause them to keep hold of their faith, Lord God.

I speak a refreshing wind over their spirit right now, Lord God, a refreshing in their heart and in their mind. I ask You to fill them with tenacity. That the strength they started with, is the strength they will finish with, and, Father, every step in between.

I speak strength; I speak tenacity; I speak power; I speak faith. Cause them to hold onto their faith and trust You that You are God and You are faithful. And so we bless you today, God.

Encourage every heart reading today, Father. I pray they would not lose their faith, God, but they would grab it with both hands and they would release the weariness, release the fatigue, and allow grace, tenacity, and strength to fill their hearts. In Jesus' Name, I pray. Amen.

You are on His Mind

"When I consider Your heavens, and the work of Your hands, the moon, and the stars, which You have ordained, what is man that You are mindful of Him, or the son of man that You visit him?"
Psalms 8:3-4 NKJV

David, the author of Psalms, marvels at God and His creation. In this verse, he says, "God, I'm looking at the sun, and the stars, and the moon, and the heavens. You made all these things God, and you ordained all these things, so what is it about mankind that You are even mindful?" In today's words, David is asking God, "How do we even make it on Your radar when You've fashioned all these spectacular things?"

I've had the opportunity to travel to many places, including Alaska, Africa, India and Mexico. I have been able to see firsthand the beauty and spectacular vistas of God's creation. Like David, I marveled. It's more than being on Your radar God. It's that You are engaged with mankind. Who is man that You would visit man? Who is man that You would send Your Son? Why would You even consider saving us? The bottom line is that the Lord loves us more than the moon, and the stars and the skies, and everything else He created.

We are the love of God's life. You, child of God, are the love of God's life. He loves you. He loves you with an everlasting love. There is nothing more precious to God than you. He's mindful of you. He knows exactly where you are right now. He knows exactly what you're walking through. He knows exactly what you need. He is mindful. His mind is on you.

David is so baffled by this. Here You are God. You're this big, amazing God who made all these things and yet, in Your mind, I take first place. I am in Your thoughts, enough to save, to walk with me, and to build a plan for my life. You are mindful of me God. You care about me and You love me.

If you think for one minute that God is not mindful of you, that is a lie from the pit of hell. God is mindful. God is concerned. God is walking with you. God has plans for you. In spite of what you feel or what you see, all that matters is what the Word says. He is mindful. He has a plan. He is with you. He loves you. It doesn't matter who doesn't love you, because there is a God who loves you greatly. He is a God that is always tender and kind with His people, and He loves you today.

I'm praying for a double portion of His love to be poured, that you would sense His love in a greater way and you would be enfolded and enveloped in His love. I pray He would take out all fear, and all rejection, and all the things that feeling unloved makes us feel, and it would be replaced with the understanding that the Creator of the universe who made the stars, and the moon, and all these other things is mindful of you. His mind is on you.

Lets Pray: Father, I pray for Your children today. I pray God, You would encourage hearts so that they would know You are for them and love them. Lord God, even as David was baffled, so are we. What is man that You are mindful, oh God, or the Son of Man that You would visit us God? And, yet You do.

You are mindful, You visit, You care, and You love. God we're so grateful for Your love. I pray You cover them in Your love and they would experience a depth of Your love as never before, God. Place Your hand upon them, Lord God. Lead them close to You and may they sense Your love in a special way. Come have Your way, in Jesus' name. Amen.

You Will Not Be Consumed

"It's because of the Lord's mercies that we are not consumed,
Because His compassions fail not.
They are new every morning; great is Your faithfulness."
Lamentations 3:22 NKJV

The word consumed is pretty dramatic. It's because of His mercy, His lovingkindness we are not consumed. Child of God, there are many things that come our way and try to consume us, destroy us, take us apart and absolutely devour us. That won't happen, because of His lovingkindness. Those things will not consume you. Even though you might feel overwhelmed and don't have any more breath, there is always that moment the Lord says that because of His lovingkindness, it will not consume you.

His mercies, don't fail. The Lord's mercies are there. They're present, and the Bible says they are new every single morning. Every morning you get up, there is fresh mercy for you. Fresh mercy, like the manna God sent down to the Israelites. Every morning, they would have fresh manna. They couldn't save manna from the day before. They couldn't stockpile it or hoard it. They had to take what they needed just for that day with the assurance that, every day, there would be fresh manna.

You too, child of God, have the same assurance that every morning, there's going to be fresh mercy, and fresh grace for whatever's going to come that day. He is going to give you the grace and the mercy to walk through it. It's because of His lovingkindness that these things aren't going to consume you.

There will be trials and circumstances. The Bible tells us that it rains on the just and the unjust. There's no way that we can avoid hard times as a believer. I wish we could. I wish that being a believer meant we were never going to see tragedies or difficult things. We will. We will see terrible things. While there's no way around it, it will not consume us. While it was meant to destroy us, it won't. The enemy sends it to take us out, but he can't. The Lord's lovingkindness will stop him.

Remember, every morning, there will be fresh grace, new mercies, and the compassion and grace of God, because His mercies they fail not. Great is His faithfulness. Our anchor is knowing that whatever we are confronted with, that's come to consume us; it cannot because our God is faithful. He is with us. He is for us and He is faithful. He does not change. He is the same yesterday, today, and forever.

It's because of His lovingkindness that we are not consumed. Because His mercies, they fail not. They are new every morning. Great is His faithfulness and we rest in His faithfulness. We recognize that though things come to break us, to hurt us, and though, at moments, we might feel utterly disheartened and broken, whatever comes, it cannot destroy us. It cannot take us out because great is His faithfulness. Our trust, our anchor, our hope sits right there in His faithfulness and His lovingkindness towards us. He can meet us in a way no one else can.

Lets Pray: I thank you Lord God, because of Your lovingkindness we are not consumed. I'm grateful that things that come our way that are meant to destroy us can't destroy us. They can't consume us. We can be injured, we can be hurt, we can be downcast God, but they will not consume us. You will walk with us, God. You will put Your lovingkindness as a barricade and every morning, You'll give us fresh mercy and fresh grace, because You're a faithful God and we rest in that anchor today. We give you praise. In Jesus' Name. Amen.

Our Covenant God

"He is the faithful God who keeps
His covenant for a thousand generations."
Deuteronomy 7:9 NKJV

I love the Old Testament. It is filled with such great truths! One great truth is found in the book of Deuteronomy. Deuteronomy 7:9 says, "He is the faithful God who keeps His covenant for a thousand generations." What I want to focus on is this word "covenant." The word covenant means that God is in partnership. We have a covenant God and we don't always fully understand what that means.

The people from the Old Testament would have partnerships where they agreed or promised certain things in writing or with the exchange of animals, cattle or land. This exchange signifies a promise, but there's a difference between promise and covenant. In the Old Testament. 'covenant' went a step further than a promise. A covenant was sealed in blood. They would kill an animal to be able to seal their covenant together.

God reminds us by saying, "I am a faithful God. I am a covenant God." This means that His promises to us were sealed with the blood of Jesus. He made a covenant with us. He sealed his promises over us. He is a faithful God who has kept us and keeps His promises to us with a covenant promise for not one generation but "for a thousand generations" according to scripture.

Look at how God's hand has been over the people of Israel even to this day. You know why? Because of a promise he made to

Abraham many years ago. He gave his word to Abraham, and he has kept that word for over 2000 years.

You know why? He's a covenant God. The Bible says that the God we serve is faithful and He keeps His covenant. He keeps the promises that He makes and that He has sealed with His blood for up to a thousand generations.

So, child of God, let me ask you a question. What are the promises of God that you're believing for? Because I want to tell you, they haven't expired. They haven't fallen to the ground. God hasn't forgotten them. You are in covenant with the Lord. The day you became His child, there was a seal put on you by His blood, and you both became a covenant relationship. He doesn't turn His back on you and He doesn't walk away. You can walk away, you can turn your back, but He will never leave you. The Bible says that He is married to the backslider. It doesn't matter how far you might feel from Him. God is exactly where He said He would be because He's a faithful God, and He keeps His covenant for a thousand generations.

So there are some of you who are looking at your children and your future and saying, "It looks so messy." The Lord is saying, "Hey, listen. My hand is over you, my partnership, my promise, and my covenant with you is not just for you. It's for a thousand generations after you." It's for generation after generation: your children, your grandchildren, your great-grandchildren. And that doesn't mean just the children that you give birth to. I have never given physical birth, but that doesn't matter. I am not left out. I have "sons" and "daughters" all around the world. That's my second generation and they will give birth to generations, and those generations will give birth to the next generation, because I serve a covenant God who is faithful.

When He makes a promise, He is faithful to His promise for a thousand generations. So I want to encourage you and I want to remind you that the God that we serve is faithful. What He says He will do, He has sealed it with His blood. We are in covenant partnership. That means nothing breaks our partnership with God. We can walk away or we can reject God, but He will never reject us. He will pursue us until the day we die.

So, if you are far from God, I want to encourage you, just turn back. Your covenant God is waiting for you. You feel distant from Him, just turn back. Your covenant God is waiting right there. He has not moved. He is faithful for a thousand generations. Turn back, He's waiting. If you need to be reminded today of His promises, of His faithfulness, be reminded that you serve a covenant God that is married to you. He has sealed His life with yours and He doesn't turn. The blood of Jesus has sealed that, and we are in partnership for a thousand generations.

Lets Pray: Father, I thank You God for Your faithfulness and for Your mercy. I thank You that we are in covenant with You Lord God, for a thousand generations. I thank You that You are a covenant God and that You have sealed us with You through the blood of Jesus. As we become Your children and accept Jesus' sacrifice on the cross, we now become covenant family with You God. I thank You that Your promises to us are not for just us, Lord God, but they will go on and on and on for a thousand generations. I thank You for Your faithfulness, Father, and I pray that everyone reading this would rest in Your faithfulness today. Great is Your name, Jesus. We give You praise in Jesus' name. In Jesus' name. Amen.

Fear and Trembling

"Therefore, my beloved as you have always obeyed,
not as in my presence only, but now much more in my absence,
work out your own salvation with fear and trembling."
Philippians 2:12 NKJV

Today's word found in Philippians 2:12, says, "therefore, my beloved as you have always obeyed, not as in my presence only, but now much more in my absence. Work out your own salvation with fear and trembling." Paul is writing to the Church and he's saying in front of me, you've acted well. You've done the right thing. You've done the God thing in front of me. Now, in my absence, do it even more. Don't do the right thing to impress me. Do the right thing because it's the right thing. Do the God thing because it's the God thing, not because I'm looking, not because people are looking, but because God is looking. Do it in my absence even better.

Now there is an interesting part. "Work out your salvation with fear and trembling." What does this say to us? As believers, are we supposed to walk around afraid and terrified to make a mistake? No, that's not it. The premise of this Scripture is that we are to be so in love with Jesus that the thought of displeasing Him would make us fearful and tremble. We should be so in love with Him that the thought of displeasing Him would make us so sick. God wants you to serve Him with all your heart. Not because man is looking at you. Not because leaders are looking at you. Not because things are going on around you. But because you want to please Him because it's the right thing. It's the thing that you know to do.

Do it in the absence of the eyes. Don't be a man pleaser. Don't do things because people are looking. Do things because you love Jesus. Do the right thing and work every day to be more like Jesus. Every day, die a little bit more to yourself to become more like Jesus. Die a little bit more to your flesh and let your spirit grow in fear and trembling.

Desire to please God. Not because He's an angry God, or because He's going to harm or hurt you, but because you love Him. When you love someone, the thought of displeasing him or her hurts you to your core. The thought of someone that you love being hurt by something you've done is so painful.

God is saying, walk that out with Me. Don't be afraid of Me because I'm going to judge you, but have fear and trembling that you're going to hurt Me by your actions. Do the right thing. Do the God thing and you know at what cost? At all cost. Do it not because someone's watching, not because there are eyes on you but because you love Jesus and you want to emulate Him, look like Him, even when no one is looking. Don't worry about what eyes are looking at you. Don't worry about who's watching you. It could be the Apostle Paul, it doesn't matter. Do it unto the Lord with fear and trembling.

We are saved, but we are not sanctified. We are being sanctified every day. We are growing every day. Or we should be growing every day. Every day, with fear and trembling, walk out your salvation. Walk out your sanctification. Be more like Jesus every day. Not because people are watching, but because you want to please Him.

Lets Pray: Father, I pray that You would help us to walk out our salvation. Help us every day to look more and more like You, to die to ourselves and to live in You, Jesus. We ask You, God, to lead us. Guide us and help us to present ourselves to You, a living sacrifice for Your glory; not caring what eyes are on us, but caring only that we please You. We give You all things today,

Lord. Help us every day to look more and more like You. In Jesus' Name. Amen.

Even the Wind and Waves

"He calms the storm, so that its waves are still."
Psalms 107:29 NKJV

There's a story in Scripture where the disciples are going through a storm. Jesus was on the boat with them and He told them, "Go to the other side." He fell asleep, and a storm broke out and the disciples (who are fishermen) became terrified. You have to wonder what the storm looked like that even fishermen are scared! Fishermen see storms all the time. A storm for them is not a big deal. When fishermen are scared, it must be quite a storm.

They forgot that Jesus told them they're going to make it to the other side. They forgot His word. You see His word was greater than the storm they were facing. Whatever you walk through, His word is greater than the storm you are facing. It doesn't matter what's in front of you. It just matters who is with you. Psalms 107:29 says, "He calms the storm, so that its waves are still." The Lord Himself calms the storm, so even the waves stand still. There are two things God can do. He can calm the storm or He can walk you through the storm. Either way, child of God, victory belongs to you. It doesn't matter what you're facing. All that matters is that God is with you. He is present with you and walking with you. You are not walking alone.

Whatever the storm is in front of you, whatever the waves look like, whatever the wind looks like, even if you're in a storm that would scare you the way the storm scared the fishermen, don't be afraid because He's with you. He is able to calm the storm. He's even given you the authority to speak to the winds and the waves and to command them to be still.

Many times, on missions trips, we would see unbelievable weather. My team and I would raise our hands, rebuke the clouds and the storm, and we would watch it dissipate right in front of our eyes. Every year, we had a children's event at one of the churches I pastored, and, every year, the week that we were going to have our event, rainstorms or thunderstorms were always predicted. Every year, we would rebuke the storms in the name of Jesus. Not only did we not have the weather they predicted each year, but there would be a rainbow as a mark over the ministry.

Do you know why? Because we have authority. Whatever storm you're physically walking through, you have authority. Whatever storm you're spiritually walking through, you have authority. The same way the Lord is able to calm the winds and the storm, you, child of God, can declare the Word of God and watch those winds and storms be put to sleep. Even if they don't get put to sleep and you have to walk through them, it's okay, because I promise you that you will get through it.

Victory belongs to the household of faith. It is synonymous with the name of Jesus. So today be encouraged. Whatever storm you're walking through, victory has been granted to you. The Lord will either stop the storm or He'll walk you through the storm. Either way, child of God, you're going to make it through to the other side.

Lets Pray: I pray for everyone reading, that whatever storm they're walking through, God, encourage their heart. Father, I speak to these storms in the name of Jesus. Every single one, I command them now in the name of Jesus to dissipate before their eyes. I pray that You would speak to these waves and these storms and they would decrease, they would stop, they would cease. Just as Your Word says, You will calm the storms in front of us and even the waves will be still. I pray, God, You would give everyone whose reading strength in their heart, courage in their mind and the understanding that whether You stop the storm or You walk them through the storm, victory belongs to them.

Walk with them I pray. Anoint them, cover them with Your blood and let a tenacious heart rise up in them that You are with them and You are for them. Even the wind and the waves have to obey Your voice. We thank You for the authority You've given us as Your children. We stand on it today in Jesus' Name. Amen.

Jesus + Nothing = Everything

"For unto us a child is born, Unto us a Son is given;
And the government will be upon His shoulder.
And His name will be called Wonderful Counselor, Mighty God,
Everlasting Father, Prince of Peace."
Isaiah 9:6 NKJV

In this one verse, Isaiah 9:6, is everything that we need. When Jesus came, He came to give us everything. He came to be the fulfillment of every promise that God spoke. God had put all these prophecies in place, all these things about how He was going to restore and rebuild the world, and Jesus was the fulfillment of all those things.

Today in your life, Jesus is still the fulfillment of all these things. I love this saying. I say it all the time: "Jesus plus nothing equals everything." I don't know what your week looks like, or even what the year holds for you. I do know that whatever you need, Jesus is able to meet that need. If you need Him to be the Prince of Peace, He's present. If you need Him to be your Counselor, He's present. If you need a Mighty Father, Jesus is present. If you need Him to speak peace into your dark place, He's present. If you need Him to comfort your heart, He's present.

Jesus plus nothing equals everything. He is Emmanuel, God with us, walking with us, being with us, living with us. Can I tell you that you are never alone? You never have to feel alone. Jesus is with you. He is walking with you. He is speaking to you. He is instructing you. You are not alone, child of God.

We celebrate that Jesus came into this world to redeem the world, and that the King of Kings, Lord of Lords, Prince of Peace, Everlasting Father and Wonderful Counselor has come to fulfill everything in your life. Know that God is a God who keeps His Word. The first promise of Jesus came to Adam and Eve. From that day to this day, God has never, never gone back on His Word. If He's given you a word, He's going to cause it to come to pass, the same way He caused Jesus to come to pass, to fulfill all His Words.

Today, He's your healer. He's your deliverer. He's your God. He's your advocate. He's your defender. He is your best friend. I encourage you today, know that unto us a Son was given, a child was given and the government is going to be upon His shoulder. He will be the reigning King and there will be no King higher than Jesus. He is the King of Kings and the Lord of Lords. Today, you get to walk with Him. You get to have Him in your life, leading and guiding. Lean in with everything you have in you. Let Him be your Wonderful Counselor, your Mighty God, your Prince of Peace, your Everlasting Father. Lean into Him and let Him be Lord of every area of your life.

Lets Pray: Father, I pray for any heart that's discouraged today. God, I speak life in the name of Jesus. I speak encouragement. I speak strength, Lord God. I pray You would be illuminated in every heart and every mind, God. I pray that you would increase and everything else decrease. Jesus, we stand eternally grateful for what You've done and, today, we make You the Lord and King of our life, in every area of our life. Come Lord, have Your way. God, we give You praise in Jesus' name. Amen.

Stranger Danger

*"The sheep follow Him, for they know His voice,
Yet they will by no means follow a stranger, but will flee from him, for they do not know the voice of strangers."*
John 10:4,5 NKJV

When we were children, we learned this saying, "stranger danger." That saying was meant to keep us from harm. The Scripture we are looking at today is meant to do the same thing! Jesus is teaching us that His sheep know His voice, and the voice of a stranger they will not follow. It's so important to understand that we, the children of God, have the ability to hear God's voice. Oftentimes, people say to me, "Well, I can't hear God." That's a lie from the enemy. Any child of God can hear their Shepherd speaking.

We may get confused about how God speaks. We think most times, God speaks in this very audible voice. There are clearly times in Scripture where there is an audible voice of God. Even in my personal life, I have heard God audibly on numerous occasions, but that's not the main way He speaks. He speaks mostly through His Word. He also speaks through promptings in our hearts: a peace, a leading, a guiding. There are times I may feel this trepidation in my spirit, and I know it's God trying to warn me or move me away.

Other times, I may hear a word, or I'll get a sense. God will speak to me in many ways, and I know His voice. I've learned His voice. The Scripture says, "My sheep," which we are, "can hear their Shepherd." Our Shepherd is Jesus. He is the good Shepherd, and He constantly speaks to His people. We, His sheep, will hear His voice because we know Him, and the voice of the stranger we will not follow because we don't recognize it.

There are hundreds of voices speaking to you: TV, social media, friends, family, jobs, etc. Sometimes the biggest voice that's speaking to you is your own. Child of God, you have to learn that the loudest voice in your life has to be the voice of the Lord. It has to be louder even than your own voice. Your own voice is that voice of reason, that voice of understanding, that voice that says, "I've got this all figured out." You can't even follow that voice. That voice can't lead you. The voice that has to lead you is the voice of the Lord Jesus Christ. His voice, your good Shepherd's voice, has to be the loudest voice in your life, and sometimes His loud voice is a whisper. It's a whisper.

How do you hear Him?

You need to learn how to shut things down. You need to learn to quiet things around you, so you can hear God as He's speaking to you, as He's directing you. That's a very intentional thing, child of God, that you have to learn to do. You have to learn to tune in to the voice of God. It doesn't mean that God can't break through all the noise to speak to you. He can. He's done it for me. He'll do it for you, but, most times, you have to quiet things around you. You have to learn to listen to the whisper of God as He's speaking to you.

His voice needs to be the loudest voice in your life. You have to seek it out. You have to look for it. It has to matter to you to hear His voice, for Him to direct you, for Him to speak to you, because you're His sheep. Once you begin to hear the voice of God and you're intentional about listening for the voice of God, you'll hear it more and more often, and you won't recognize the voice of the stranger. You'll wait to hear God speak to you and instruct you.

Truly, He wants to speak to you. He doesn't want to leave you in the fog. He doesn't want to leave you without direction. He doesn't want to leave you without an answer. God wants to speak to you. Do you want to listen? Do you want to hear Him? If the answer is yes, child of God, start tuning in so that He can speak to you and His voice can be the loudest voice in your life.

Lets Pray: Father, I pray for Your children, that they would tune their spiritual ears to Your voice, Lord God. I pray Father they would learn to shut out all the other voices and tune into Your voice and to Your heart Lord God. They would learn the sound of Your voice, and as good sheep they will follow. Lord, I pray they would not follow the voice of the stranger; they won't even recognize it. They would know Your voice. Have Your way in their life in Jesus' Name. Amen.

Grace and Purity!

"He who loves purity of heart and has grace on his lips, the king will be his friend."
Proverbs 22:11 NIV

I wanted to share a verse with you found in Proverbs 22:11. It says, "He who loves purity of heart and has grace on his lips, the king will be his friend." I love this verse. It's so powerful and it's such a picture for how the body of Christ should look and how we should look as believers. "He who loves purity of heart" really has to do with he who sees people in a pure way; he who looks at people and circumstances with the purity of Christ.

That means I'm always looking at people and looking at things in a redemptive way because that's God. God is redemptive. God doesn't throw people away and He doesn't throw things away. God looks at things as redemptive. "How do I redeem?" That is purity of heart.

We're certainly not that way all the time, but, if we love to redeem things, love to work things out for God's glory, love purity of heart and have grace on our lips, even the king can be our friend! This is maybe even more difficult than having purity of heart because grace on your lips means that what you say is redemptive and not harmful. The book of James says that the most evil thing we possess is our tongue, and that if we can tame our tongue, then we're perfect.

So that means your tongue has incredible power. Your words have incredible power. Here the scripture is saying, "you who can have grace flowing out of your mouth – you have grace on your lips." What you say needs to be seasoned with grace and with mercy and with the things of God. By doing this, you don't speak death, you speak life.

That person, that person who has that purity of heart, who looks at things with redemption, that looks at things to win for the kingdom and looks at things with purity and grace on their tongue, is a person who, with the power of their tongue, brings life and not death.

The Bible says that the king will be a friend to the person who loves purity of heart and has grace on his lips. That means they will be able to speak to the greatest authority and win. The king will look at them as a friend, as a peer, because that person will stand out.

Today, I don't know your life and I don't know what you may be walking through. But, I want you to know that, today, you can be somebody who walks in favor.

You can walk in favor with any authority. You can walk in favor in your life if you learn these two principles, "how I walk with a pure heart," and "how I walk with grace on my tongue?" As I mentioned earlier, our tongues are so dangerous. So, oftentimes, some of the greatest things we can do about our tongue is say nothing until we can say something with grace.

Hold back our tongues until we can say something with grace. Hold back and let your heart be filtered by the Lord. Let that purity of God come into your heart and say, "God, how do I judge this? How do I look at this circumstance with purity, God? Because, now, I'm tainted." We all have these filters around our life and these filters cause us to see things a certain way.

Our filters look like: how we were raised, how we understand things, how we've been hurt, etc. So, we use these filters and filter everything through them and that makes our hearts not pure because we've walked through different things. If you walk through a lot of rejection, you filter everything through rejection. If you've walked through a lot of abandonment, you filter everything through abandonment. God is saying, "Bring that back to me. Let me wash that out so you can have purity of heart."

Fill your heart with the word of God. You want to talk about something that washes your heart and makes it pure? The word of God is primal. Let it wash your heart. Let it make your heart pure so that when you look at a circumstance, you're looking with His eyes, you're feeling with His heart, and you're speaking with His tongue.

What would it be like if the church only spoke what God wanted us to say? The Bible says what'll happen is the king would be our friend. Any person of authority would be our friend because they would feel grace around us. They would feel purity around us. They would feel Jesus around us.

So I'm going to encourage you today, as you walk, make this a new model for your life. "I want to be pure at heart and I want to be gracious on my mouth, Lord God. I want my love to be pure at heart, and I want to have grace flowing out of my lips, so that even the king, the most evil of kings, would be my friend."

Lets Pray. Father, I pray for Your church. God, I pray that You would encourage them. I pray that they would know that You are for them and that You love them, Lord God. I pray today that You would teach them this week Father, what it is to be pure in heart and what it is to be gracious with their lips that what they speak is life-giving, Lord God. What they speak is encouraging. What they speak is from Your throne, Lord God. I pray You place Your hand upon all things, Lord God, and that Your name would be lifted up through their life. Have Your way we pray, in Jesus name. Amen and amen.

The Force of Grace

"My grace is sufficient for you,
for My strength is made perfect in weakness."
2 Corinthians 12:9 NKJV

I want to share with you from the Word of God about grace. It's really important as people of God that we understand what grace is and how grace operates. In 2 Corinthians 12:9, we read, "My grace is sufficient for you, for My strength is made perfect in weakness." What does this mean? What is grace? The grace of God is an incredible force. It is strength; it is equipping; it is ability. It is the unmerited favor of God, and that's powerful.

"So my grace is sufficient for you." The grace of God is not passive. It means that whatever you're walking through, whatever is coming upon you, the minute you open your eyes every morning, the grace of God is there. Grace sufficient for whatever the day is going to bring. His grace is sufficient.

You can never walk far enough away that God can't find you, that His grace can't find you and bring you back. His grace is sufficient. His grace is enough. It is His grace plus nothing. It is enough. It's sufficient. It's complete. Whatever's going to come your way, whatever mistakes you're going to make, whatever's going to happen, the grace of God is covering it. It's sufficient and the strength of God is made perfect in weakness.

When we are in need of grace because we're weak, making bad mistakes or struggling with sin, anxiety or fear, the Bible assures us that "His strength is made perfect in our weakness."

If, in my frailty, in my brokenness, in my weakness, in my struggle, I turn to God and I am honest with Him, His strength comes in with grace and power and makes me strong in that weakness. His grace comes because I've acknowledged my need of Him. I've admitted I cannot do this without Him. I can't overcome these things without Him. It is in that weakness, His strength is made perfect.

As long as I'm strong and I don't need the grace of God, or think I don't need the grace of God, the Bible says "God resists the proud." That attitude is pride. God resists the proud, but He gives grace to the humble. When I am proud and don't need God and I have this figured out, then God will resist me. The moment I'm humble and say, "God, I need You. I am in need of Your strength. I am in need of Your Spirit. I am in need of Your forgiveness, God," then His strength comes in. He gives me grace because I've humbled myself. His grace provides the ability to endure, to succeed and to thrive. His grace is sufficient for anything I'm walking through, for anything that's going on in my life.

His grace is active and available, child of God. Grab hold of it today. Resist being proud. Be humble and let the grace of God fill you and know that in your weakest moments. His strength is made perfect there and His grace is sufficient.

Lets Pray: Father, I pray for Your people, I pray God that You would allow Your grace to saturate them today. Let them know that whatever is coming their way; Your grace is sufficient for them. It is more than enough, Lord God, and in their weakness, in their frailty as they turn to You, they are made strong. And so Father, we thank You for Your strength. We thank You for Your power. Thank You for Your anointing. We thank You, God, that nothing's going to come our way that Your grace is not enough for. There's nothing that's going to come our way that Your grace cannot defeat, Lord God. Your grace is sufficient, and we receive it and we walk in it. In Jesus' Name. Amen.

Not by Might

"Not by might, nor by power,
but by My Spirit, says the Lord of hosts."
Zechariah 4:6 NKJV

Sometimes, there are words that truly just bubble in my spirit. Zechariah 4:6 is one of them! Here the Lord is talking to Israel as they're getting ready to go into battle and trying to figure out a battle plan. And the verse that the Lord speaks to them is "Not by might, nor by power, but by My Spirit, says the Lord of hosts." This world teaches us that you've got to go for yours, and you've got to grab what you want. There's so much truth in that! But, there are things that are not going to move by your might or by your power. They're going to move because the Spirit of the Lord has moved them.

"Not by might, nor by power, but by My Spirit, says the Lord". So we can try everything we can to make things move. There are some of you who have been praying for people to change, praying for spouses to change or children to change, and you're looking for the right word or the right opportunity. You keep knocking on every door because you're trying to do it by your might and you're trying to do it by your power, but what really has the power to change that person or that circumstance is the Spirit of the Lord—He does the work.

What is your posture now when you're understanding that? It's not by my might. It's not because I pushed enough. It's not because I'm strong enough. It's not because I have all this information and it's not because I'm educated. None of this has the power to make these things move. It's the Spirit of the Lord that's going to make them move.

So, what is my posture now? My posture is prayer, faithful prayer, standing, waiting and believing. That posture of just saying, "God, I'm going to be thankful for what you're going to do." It's the posture of just standing, believing and having that patience that He asks us to wait in. Then finally, the thankfulness. This posture looks like, "Lord you're in this and it's not going to move by my might. It's not going to move by my power. It's going to move by Your spirit. So I'm going to pray and create an atmosphere for Your spirit to move. I'm going to wait patiently because I know Your spirit is at work, and I'm going to thank You in advance for moving the circumstance or situation by Your spirit."

I want to encourage you today. I don't know what's in front of you. I don't know what you're walking through. But whatever your circumstances may look like today, put your heart's focus not on your own might, nor on your own power, but on the understanding that it's by the Spirit of the Lord that He will do it. Create room for the Spirit of God to move on your behalf.

Don't do it on your own. You can't do it. Ask Him to do it. Then, wait patiently and stand thankfully that He will accomplish His good work on your behalf.

Lets Pray. Father, I pray for those that are reading today. I pray for Your peace. I pray for Your grace. I pray for just faith to rise up in them, Lord God. That they would understand today deeply in their spirit, not by might, nor by power, but by Your spirit God, things are moved. We reckon into the spirit world that only Your spirit can navigate, God. And so we just create room through prayer. We create room, Lord, through our patience and we create room through our thanksgiving, believing that we have what You say, not when we see it, but when we pray. And so, we receive that today Lord God, and we thank You that everything in front of us is subject to change, but You. We give You praise today in Jesus' name, Amen.

Your Mind is Not Saved

"Do not be conformed to this world,
but be transformed by the renewing of your mind."
Romans 12:2 NKJV

How many of you know that when you got saved your mind didn't get saved? Your mind is flesh, and your mind is filled with things that are ungodly and filled with things that don't glorify Jesus. It's filled with thoughts of hatred, lust, jealousy, envy, and selfishness. That is our minds. Romans 12:2 says, "Do not be conformed to this world, but be transformed by the renewing of your mind." Our mind is in this world and it's constantly being conformed to the world around us.

Our minds are being bombarded by images and the things that people say, which is their truth and not the truth of God's word. There's this concept of everyone having a truth. There is only one truth, and that's the word of God. So our minds are constantly in this battle to be conformed to these things, but the Bible challenges you. Don't be conformed to these things. Don't look around at fleshly things and let your mind be conformed to them. Transform your mind by the renewing of your mind. How do you renew your mind? You renew your mind with the word of God. You take the word of God, and you allow the word of God to wash your mind. If you have a thought, or a feeling, or an emotion that doesn't match up to the word of God, you know what has to change? Your thoughts have to change, not the word of God. So, the word becomes the standard.

As we renew our minds with the word, there is a washing that happens and your mind transforms. Your mind begins to get sanctified and cleaned. It begins to think godly things, godly thoughts and godly perspective. But, if you are not renewing your mind on a daily basis, your mind is being conformed into this world.

There are only two choices: Either it's going to be transformed by the word of God or it's going to be conformed by the world. That remains your choice. Either the world can absorb your mind and you can begin to think worldly thoughts all the time. Or the word of God can begin to transform your thoughts and you begin to think godly thoughts.

Let me tell you something, the word of God will change you daily. Every day, the word of God has the potential to change you if you allow it to wash your mind and wash your thoughts. When you read the word of God, it's not for you to challenge. It's for you to accept and say, "God, I am in submission to Your word. I'm not here to tell You that Your word is wrong. I am here to submit to Your word because it's Your word, God. I'm going to allow it to renew my mind, and whatever is in my mind and in my thoughts that is not of You, I'm going to allow Your spirit to wash it. So now, my thoughts glorify You and everything that I think are Your thoughts, God." We need to begin to do this on a regular basis.

Let your mind be transformed by the word of God because it's going to renew you, and it's going to cause you to walk deeper and deeper into the things of God. You can be saved awalk with the Lord and not renew your mind. And as a result, you'll never walk in everything God has for you – you will walk very limited. God doesn't want that for you. God wants you to grab everything He has for you. "Do not be conformed to this world. Be transformed by the renewing of your mind."

Let's Pray. Father, I pray for Your children that You would give them the heart to seek after Your word. Father, that their minds would not be conformed to this world and that they would hate the things of this world, Lord God. They would have a detest for the things of this world. Father, I pray that You would give them a heart to transform their minds by the renewing of Your word, Lord God. I pray You'd give them an appetite for Your word and, as they read Your word, it would come alive to them.

I pray their thoughts and their hearts would be washed by Your word, and they would become the people you've called them to be in every way—on heavenly things, thinking about heavenly things and walking in a heavenly mindset. And I pray, Lord God, that every day they will grow deeper and deeper and deeper. Every day their minds will be transformed more and more and more. Have Your way in each one Father, in Jesus name. Amen.

Jesus Never Changes

"Jesus is the same yesterday, today and forever."
Hebrews 13:8 NKJV

Let's look at Hebrews 13:8 together. It' a huge revelation. "Jesus is the same yesterday, today and forever." I'm sure you're thinking, "Well yeah, what's the big deal about that?" I want you to hear it again: "Jesus is the same yesterday, today and forever." We live in a world that is so inconsistent. We live with people who are so inconsistent. As a result, it can be very hard to trust people and to trust circumstances, employers or even people who we thought were close to us. They flip-flop, change and they alter, and it can be very hard to live that way.

Oftentimes, you may find yourself living in this place of constant trepidation. You don't know who you can trust. You don't know what you can do, or you don't know how to move forward. We live in a very inconsistent world. What this verse speaks to is the core of our hearts. It doesn't matter what around us shakes or what around us moves, because the one constant thing is that Jesus does not move. He's the same yesterday, today and forever. The Jesus you knew in the past is the Jesus that'll be present today and will be present in the future. He doesn't shift. He doesn't move. He doesn't change. He doesn't alter. Neither, child of God, does His word.

What was true about Jesus in the past is true about Jesus today and will be true about Jesus tomorrow. What He spoke in the past, is what He speaks today, and what He's speaking tomorrow is all the same. The things that grieve His heart yesterday, are the things that grieve His heart today and will grieve His heart tomorrow. What broke His heart today will break His heart tomorrow. What He promised yesterday, He promises today and He promises tomorrow – He doesn't shift.

There's nothing about Jesus that's flip-floppy. There's nothing about Jesus that's fickle. He is clear. He is the same yesterday, today and forever. He's going to be exactly who He always was. He is the same. He does not change.

What that tells me and you is that we can completely 1000% trust Him. We can put our hearts and lives in His hand and trust that He's not going to alter, change or shift. He is the same. The same love, the same care. The scripture says that He loved us while we were in our worst condition as sinners. So that means He loves me today and He'll love me tomorrow. Nothing alters His love for me. He's the same. What does it tell me about His word? It's the same. What does it tell me about walking with Him? It's the same. What does it tell me about trusting Him? It's the same.

Nothing alters who Jesus is. His character is flawless. It doesn't shift. It doesn't move. He is the same. So when I pray, when I talk to Him, when I walk through something, I can walk with the assurance of knowing that I know who He is. He's not going to step out of character on me and I'm not going to be like, "who is He?" I know exactly who He is because He's revealed Himself in His word, and He's revealed Himself in our relationship with Him. So what we know in the past about Jesus, is what we know today about Jesus, and what we're going to know tomorrow about Jesus.

How much confidence does that give you today, child of God? How much safety does that give you?

How much trust do you have that those arms that held you in your worst moment in the past, will hold you in your worst moment today, and will hold you in your worst moment in the future?

How much confidence does it give you to know that the God you trusted in the past to make a way for you, is the God you can trust today and tomorrow to make a way for you?
He doesn't shift. He doesn't alter. He doesn't change. You can bet your last dollar on who God is today.

So I want to encourage your heart today. Trust God a thousand million percent because He doesn't change. You know Him. He's revealed through His word. You can trust Him. You can walk with Him yesterday, today and forever.

Let's Pray. Father, I pray that Your children would be encouraged, Lord God. That You would place Your hands upon them God and that You would remind them that You are the same. You don't shift; You don't change. You are the God that stands with us yesterday, today and forever. Your love is the same yesterday, today and forever. Your power is the same yesterday, today and forever. You don't get weaker. You don't get defeated. Nothing changes You Jesus. You're the same.

So, today, with all confidence, we place our lives in Your hands knowing that we can trust Your character. We can trust Your heart and we can trust Your word knowing that it doesn't change. It doesn't alter. The whole world can shift. The whole world can be inconsistent, but You are never inconsistent. And so, we ask You God to give us the confidence to walk in that place of understanding that You don't change. You don't shift. There's nothing fickle about You. You walk with us 1000% and so we in turn can walk with You 1000%. We bless You Jesus. Amen.

God's Plan is Always Good

"For I know the plans I have for you, says the Lord, plans of good and not of evil, plans to bless you and not to harm you, plans to give you hope and a future."
Jeremiah 29:11 NIV

I want to speak to you from my favorite verse found in Jeremiah 29:11. Jeremiah 29:11 says, "For I know the plans I have for you, says the Lord, plans of good and not of evil, plans to bless you and not to harm you, plans to give you hope and a future." If you're ever concerned about what's going on in your life, if you're ever concerned about where God is and what's going on, I want you to tap into His character and I want you to tap into what this verse is saying. The scripture is saying that God has good plans concerning you, "plans to bless you and not to harm you, plans to give you hope and a future." When you read this verse, and you hear this verse, there is a revelation of the heart of God for you.

Oftentimes, things may happen in our life that don't look good. They may look harmful, they may look out of sorts, or they may look bizarre. But, the Lord is saying, "Don't worry about that. My plan, My ultimate plan, is for your good." Sometimes we have to walk through some junk to get to the good, and that's okay. Just keep walking. That's the deal.

It's like, "God, I understand that maybe what is happening right now doesn't feel good. I don't assess it as good, but, ultimately, it's going to lead to my good. I'm going to trust your character as

I walk through this because your word says that Your plan for me is good. "I want to encourage you today that the Lord's plan for your life is good. It's to bless you, not to harm you.

God's heart is always to bless His people. He's never against you, child of God. Even when He disciplines you, He's for you. He's always for you. He's always working on your behalf. He is always there "to bless you and not to harm you, to give you hope and a future." Do you know that we live in a hopeless society that just can't hope for the next day? They can't believe for the next day. And the Lord is saying, "I'm here to give you hope and a future."

You do not have to worry about tomorrow. God's got tomorrow. He's got it deeply, He's holding it. He's securing it for you, and all you have to do is believe Him and walk with faith in what He has for you. "I know the plans I have for you," says the Lord, "plans of good and not of evil." If evil comes your way, understand God didn't bring it, because that's not His plan.

His plan is good. It's to bless you. Now, can He use the negative things that happen to us? Absolutely He does, but He doesn't bring evil. That's not His heart. His heart is to always bring good. His heart is to bring favor into your life. Read the verse again "I know the plans I have for you, says the Lord, plans of good and not of evil, plans to bless you and not to harm you, plans to give you hope and a future." In that verse alone, you can rest, you can be at peace, you can be secure, you can be confident. You can be confident that God's character is good and faithful. He is our hope and He secures the things of our future.

So I want you to rest in that confidence today. I want you to walk with that assurance deep in your heart knowing that God is for you, and that He's working all things together for you, for your good, for your benefit, in order to give you hope and a future. I want you to be encouraged. I want you to walk with a pep in your step, recognizing that the Lord is for you and He's working good on your behalf. He's working hope and a future and He is never out to harm you or hurt you. We serve a good God.

Lets Pray. Father, for your children today, I pray that they'd be encouraged. I pray that they'd be strengthened. I pray Lord, that they would know, without a shadow of a doubt, that Your heart is good towards them, that Your heart is faithful towards them, that You have plans of hope and a future for them, Lord God. And Father, I pray they'd walk confidently in what You have for them for Your glory, in Jesus' name. Amen and amen.

The Weapons of Our Warfare

"The weapons of our warfare are not carnal."
2 Corinthians 10:4 NKJV

Child of God, we are at war! We have an enemy who wants to harm us, but God has prepared us for the warfare! He has even given us weapons for this battle; however, they are not the weapons that might naturally come to mind. In 2 Corinthians 10:4, the Bible tells us, "The weapons of our warfare are not carnal but mighty in God for pulling down strongholds." The enemy is not going to just stand back and let you get everything God has for you unopposed. Our warfare takes place when the things of darkness come at us, the things that try and hinder what God is trying to do.

So we shouldn't see it as a fight in the flesh. We fight a different kind of fight. It is a fight in the spirit! Therefore, the weapons of our warfare are not carnal. I don't stand there and deal naturally with things that are going on around me. No. I step into the supernatural because the weapons of my warfare are not carnal. They're not fleshly weapons, but they're mighty to the pulling down of strongholds. The strongholds that stop us from receiving everything God has for us can be pulled down.

When you learn how to fight properly in the spirit, you begin to learn what it is to stand in the things of the spirit. You need to begin to learn what it is to declare the Word of God. You need to begin to understand what it is to fight with the Sword of the Spirit, which is the Word of God. You need to begin to pray, to declare, to take authority over what God has for you and position yourself in the place that God has you and stand poised and ready for warfare.

Put on the weapons of warfare, which are the Word of God, the word of faith, the ability to pray and to declare and seek authority over the things of darkness this will allow you to begin to step forward into the things God has for you. There was a young man that I the opportunity to minister to who was possessed, truly demon possessed. When we were praying for this young man, the evil spirit kept saying, "I'm not going to let him go. I'm not letting him go." I just simply said to the spirit, "I'm not asking you. I'm not debating with you. You have no authority. I am a child of God. I have the authority. You need to go." The young man left completely delivered and set free. Do you know why? Because we are the children of God, and the weapons of our warfare are not carnal, but they are mighty to the pulling down of strongholds. The enemy cannot defeat the children of God when we stand properly, declare properly, speak properly, and pray properly, and when we understand the authority we've been given as a child of God.

When opposition comes against what God is trying to do, remember, the weapons of our warfare are not carnal, they are mighty for the pulling down of strongholds. Stand in your victory. Know that you fight from victory, not for victory. You've already been granted the victory so walk in everything God has for you. Be expecting. God has great things for you.

Lets Pray: Father, I thank You that victory belongs to Your house. I pray, God, that You would teach us how to use the weapons of our warfare for Your glory, Lord God. Thank you for your anointing that is over us, and for teaching us how to war and how to extend the authority that You've given us as Your children. Father, I thank You, Lord God, that the sky's the limit! Amen.

Roar Back at Fear

"but mighty in God for pulling down strongholds."
2 Timothy 1:7 NKJV

Fear is a very crippling spirit. Oftentimes, you see people in the church, people in the kingdom who are so afraid, they're bound by fear. They're bound by fear in many areas. They're bound by fear about the future, by a doctor diagnosis, or by things going on in their life. They just live their life afraid.
There are certain areas in their life they turned over to fear.

You need to recognize that God has not given us a spirit of fear. You need to focus in on that sentence. God has not given us a spirit of fear. If God didn't give us a spirit of fear, then who gave us a spirit of fear? The enemy; the enemy gave us a spirit of fear. God has not given us a spirit of fear, but of power, love, and a sound mind. If you are operating in fear, if you are bound by fear, if there are areas in your life that fear is dominating, understand that you've accepted something from the enemy, not from God. God has given us a spirit of power, love, and a sound mind. The enemy has given us a spirit of fear.

Your job, child of God, is to reject and push away anything that the enemy brings you. You are not to accept it in your life. Fear is not of God. You are called to live a fearless, bold, brave life. You are not called to walk in fear. You need to recognize that when fear begins to crawl near you, it's the enemy trying to put something on you. You need to learn to reject the spirit of fear.

Do you know how you reject the spirit of fear? The opposite of fear is one word; it's the word faith. Faith is the opposite of fear. In order to resist the spirit of fear, I need to come at it with the spirit of faith and say, "No, I do not receive this lie." Fear is receiving a lie from the enemy about either a situation we're walking through or going to walk through, or something that's going on in our life. When we accept his lie, we are really rejecting the love of God.

Scripture tells us "perfect love casts out all fear." If there is an area in my life that I'm operating in fear, it's because I have not fully embraced God's love for me. I don't understand it, because if I truly understand God's love for me, I wouldn't fear anything. I've accepted the lie of the enemy, that God might not love me enough in this particular area therefore, now I'm afraid.

The moment fear comes barking near you, you need to begin to reject it with faith saying, "I know I serve a good God. I know I serve a faithful God. I know I serve a righteous God and He's got me. He's given me the spirit of power and the spirit of love; He's given me a sound mind."

Do you know what a sound mind means?

It means stability, peace, and tranquility. I don't have to panic about things going on around me. He's given me a spirit of a sound mind. He's given me the spirit of love. He's given me the spirit of power.

Fear comes knocking often. We're afraid of a diagnosis, we're afraid of things going on around us, or we're afraid when we watch the news. We need to learn, as children of God, fear does not belong in the DNA of a believer. It is not part of who we are. We are not made to be afraid. We are called to be a fearless people. We're called to be courageous, bold people.

He hasn't given us a spirit of fear. He's given us a spirit of power, love, and a sound mind. Let's begin to live the fearless life that God has called us to live. I challenge you to be bold. I challenge you to be courageous. I challenge you to recognize you are completely and totally loved by the Most High God, and there is no area in your life that He is not sovereign over. There's not an area in your life you need to fear. God's got you.

He's faithful, and He just wants you to embrace Him. He wants you to walk with Him. When fear comes barking your way, you bark right back at it with faith. You manifest your faith over fear. Remember, fear and faith grow the same way.

Fear grows by believing the lies of the enemy and dwelling on lies. Faith grows by believing the truth of God's word and dwelling on His truth. It's the same pattern. It just comes down to your choice. Today, recognize fear is not of God and fear doesn't belong in your DNA. Rebuke it, push through it, roar back at it with faith, and watch what God will do in your life.

Lets Pray: Father, we give You praise today. I thank You that fear does not belong in the DNA of your children. Father, I pray over them, that if they struggle with fear, that they would rebuke it and send it back to the pit of hell from where it came because we recognize You have not given us a spirit of fear. You've given us a spirit of power, love, and a sound mind, and I speak strength. I ask faith to rise up, Lord God. I ask courage to rise up in every heart, Lord God, that we would be the fearless people You've called us to be and that we always respond to fear with faith.

Make us a people of faith that You've called us to be. And Father, we're so grateful You respond to faith, and that Your Word says You are eager to please those that step out in faith. And so Father, we refuse, refuse to be prisoners of fear. We call ourselves a fearless generation for Your glory. We give You praise in Jesus' Name. Amen.

Burn or Build, Your Choice!

"A soft answer turns away wrath, but a harsh word stirs up anger."
Proverbs 15:1 NKJV

Words are so powerful! They have the power to burn or build. The choice is yours! Proverbs 15:1 tells us, "A soft answer turns away wrath, but a harsh word stirs up anger." Conflict is a normal part of life. You have to decide with every conflict whether you want to build a bridge or whether you want to burn a bridge. People say words are even more powerful than bullets. You can heal from different physical wounds, but words can cut so deeply they can scar people for a lifetime.

Scripture teaches us that when someone is coming at you with wrath, your answer, your choice at that moment, is to either stir up anger with a harsh word or respond with a soft answer and diffuse the situation. You have that ability as a child of God. You have the Word of God; you have the power of the Holy Spirit to decide in that moment how to react, how to respond. We're going to have conflict as a normal part of life, but we need to decide with every conflict, with every issue, whether we want to build a bridge or burn a bridge. Will my harsh answer stir up wrath and worsen the situation? There now is a burnt bridge in front of me that God has to miraculously touch.

My alternative is to answer with the love of God. I can answer with grace. I can answer with humility. While no one likes to eat humble pie, it's God's way. Answering with humility, grace and love is the Bible alternative. Another verse says that a soft response causes a bucket of cold water on the head of the person coming at you. They don't know what to do with that soft answer. They're expecting a 'flesh' answer, a harsh or angry word. If we act like Jesus and we return it with a soft answer, there's grace and that person's anger is diffused. Then, child of God, you've built a bridge, not burned it. As you read the Word of God, let it penetrate your heart, so when you are confronted with conflict, you will remember that a soft answer turns away wrath, but a harsh word will stir up anger.

The book of Proverbs also teaches us that the power of life and death is in the tongue. Decide by your tongue, by your actions, am I going to be a builder of bridges or am I going to be a burner of bridges? I pray you choose to build bridges because truly as children of God, we are ministers of reconciliation. Our job is to build bridges and bring reconciliation and peace as agents for the Most High God.

Lets Pray: Lord, teach us to build with our words and not burn. Help us to control our words and always use them to speak life! In Jesus' name. Amen.

Living in Peace

"If it is possible, as much as depends on you, live peaceably with all men."
Romans 12:18 NIV

Before we read from the Book of Romans, I want you to have some context for our verse. We have this incredible opportunity to have a relationship with the Lord and to walk with God on a daily basis, but your relationship with the Lord is not an exclusive relationship between you and God. Your relationship with the Lord should transcend all your relationships. The fruit of your relationship with the Lord should be felt in your marriage, with your friends, with your family, with your coworker. It should pour into every other relationship in your life. There should be fruit of your walk with God in those relationships. There should be evidence of your walk with God in those relationships.

In Romans chapter twelve verse eighteen it says, "If it is possible, as much as depends on you live peaceably with all men."

What does that tell me?

It tells me there's going to be conflict. We're going to have plenty of conflict in our lives. There may be people we're not going to naturally fit together with, or people we had relationships with and things went sour. There are going to be issues. There's going to be conflict. There's going to be people who actually hurt you.

The verse right before that says, "Do not repay evil for evil." There are people who are actually going to do evil things to you. They're going to come at you to harm you or hurt you.The Scripture says, "As much as it depends on you, live at peace with all men."

What does that mean?

It's incumbent upon you as a child of God, who has a relationship with the Lord, to do what's best to be at peace, be a peacemaker. Be someone who seeks out grace and peace. Be someone that looks to resolve conflicts, not to blow them up.

We, as believers, walk around with two buckets, one with gasoline and the other with water. We have a choice when we're dealing with people to either throw gasoline on the situation and explode the situation, or throw water on it and diffuse it.The Scripture says, "As much as depends on you, as much as you are responsible, live at peace with all men." Find a way to be a peacemaker. That doesn't mean don't deal with issues. Definitely deal with issues, confront issues and deal with things that hurt you. Don't allow people to mistreat you. Deal with them; but also look to redeem, look to resolve, look to heal. Look to be at peace with all men.

It says, "As much as depends on you be at peace with all men." The other piece we need to understand is "As much as depends on you." This tells me, you're not going to be at peace with all men. There are people that you're not going to be at peace with because it's not all dependent on you. It depends on someone else. It depends on someone else's point of view. It depends if that person wants to be at peace with you. If they don't, no matter what you do, it will not change the situation. At that point, you bless them.

If you've done your best before God to be at peace with all men and someone doesn't want peace with you, it's okay to bless them in the Name of Jesus, do not hold any resentment, do not hold unforgiveness, do not avoid them, do not try to harm them. The Bible says, "Bless those that persecute you. Pray for them." Pray for them, but it's okay at that point to release them and say, "God, I've done everything I know to do to be at peace with this person. They don't want to have peace with me; I release it to you and trust you to meet this situation."

However, if you are not at peace with the majority of your situations, and not at peace with people, and there is friction in your home and job, you need to take a real good look inside and say, "Lord, what part of me am I not surrendering to you? What part of our relationship, God, is not transcending into my other relationships?" If there's conflict everywhere you go, you need to take a look and say, "God, how do I be at peace with all men?"

I want to encourage you to let your relationship with the Lord transcend all your other relationships. This requires you to dig a little deeper and say, "God, how do I live graciously with people? How do I look like You in my relationships? How do I sound like You? How do I care for people that are sometimes very difficult?"

People are not easy. People are difficult. People are harsh. People try to hurt us. The question then becomes, how do I look like Jesus when I deal with them? How do I serve people who want to hurt me? How do I care for people who have chosen to despise me? What do I do, God?

And God says, "As much as depends on you, be at peace with them. Don't repay evil for evil. Do it my way."

Lets Pray: Father, we pray today, God, that You would give us Godly wisdom, that You would give us understanding, that You would teach us how to treat people the way we should treat them, Lord God. Father, teach us how to deal with conflict in a Godly, healthy way. Help us Father, not to shy away from conflict or run from it, God, but help us know how to deal with it as your children. Help us not to repay evil for evil, Lord God. Help us to overcome evil with good, Lord God. Help us today, God, to do as much as depends on us to be at peace with all men. Then help us to know God, when to release and walk away and just bless them, because we've done everything we know to do. We asked you, God, to help us today, to be the children and the people that You've called us to be. In Jesus' Name we pray. Amen.

Walk with the Wise

"He who walks with the wise, he himself will be wise. But the company of fools shall be destroyed."
Proverbs 13:20 NKJV

I want to share with you today from Proverbs 13:20. In Proverbs 13:20 the bible, says, "He who walks with the wise, he himself will be wise. But the company of fools shall be destroyed." This verse should be really simple and self-explanatory; however we need to consider who we surround ourselves with has a lot to do with our spiritual growth. If we surround ourselves with people that are not spiritually hungry or people that are not wise in the things of God and people who are not ahead of us in this race then we can become very stagnant.

You see each one has a race before us that God has put in place. We can run the race and win or we can fail. If we surround ourselves with people that are foolish, we can ourselves then become foolish.The Bible says, "He who walks with the wise, he himself will become wise." Why? Because the wisdom that's coming from the person that you're walking with now begins to fill you. Not only does it begin to fill you but it begins to encourage you, it begins to incite you. It begins to say, "Hey, I want to be like them. I want to grow like them." You begin to receive wisdom.

Wisdom is imparted to you from the wise.But just like wisdom is imparted, foolishness can also be imparted. Foolishness is imparted when you surround yourself with people that don't speak life, with people that speak doubts, or with people who don't believe the things that you believe. I'm not saying don't witness to them, but you can't surround yourself with them.They can be visitors to your house. They can't be people that stay there. They can be part of your company, but they can't be your confidants, or your friends.

The people that speak into your life need to be people of godly wisdom. They need to be people of understanding. They need to be people that are in the word that can bring you along in the race.Find people that are ahead of you in the race. Find people that know the word better than you. Find people that pray more than you do. Find people that understand healing and freedom and the things of God more than you do. Why? Because that will ignite a fire. Fire is contagious. When you put yourself around people that are on fire for God, you yourself will catch fire.

On the contrary, if you surround yourself with people that are foolish, nominal in their faith, believers that are argumentative or critical, gossipers, people who are critical about the people of God, the church, or pastors and these kinds of things--that's foolish. The Bible calls that foolishness. As a matter of fact, that's even sin. You surround yourself with people like that, you will become like them.

You're called to surround yourself around people that are wise. People that can pray and people that can hear and operate in the things of the Kingdom and then bring you along for the journey. In proverbs its says, "He who walks with the wise, he himself will become wise. With the company of fools, will come to destruction." Don't be in the company of fools.

Surround yourself with those that are wise, those that can bring you up in the things of God, those that you can pray with. Not people that you can share things that are base and flesh and then just stay there.You want people that'll hear those things and then pull you higher. Those are the friends you want to keep and there's only a handful of them, but surround yourself with them. Surround yourself with people that can speak life and speak truth and the Bible says, you yourself will become like them.

I encourage you today to pick your friends wisely and be wiser in selecting your confidants and your counsel Surround yourself with wise people that are ahead of you in the race. They don't all have to be ahead of you, but some of them do. They can bring you along and you can grow in the things of God by leaps and bounds.

Lets Pray: Father, I give you praise today. I pray, for all those that are reading this today God, that you would encourage them and that Father, they would walk with the wise. You would surround them with people that love you, that walk after you, that know how to hear you, God. Believers that know how to speak life and speak a word. I pray that you'd anoint them. Lord, I pray for the people who maybe in this season and may not know how to befriend others, I pray you would bring wise Godly people around them. I pray that you draw them close to those people, Lord God, and you help them make those friendships.I pray that you would remove from our lives things that are toxic, Lord God. Things that eat away at our faith, even people that are toxic, God. That you'd move them away, Lord God. So that Father, we would be light in souls. I pray that our company of friends and our company of confidants,   are filled with people that are wise. and those that are ahead of us in the race, so they can bring us along. They can show us the way. In Jesus name, Amen!

His Desire is My Desire

"Hope deferred makes the heart sick, but when the desire comes, it is a tree of life."
Proverbs 13:12 NKJV

Today's verse is in Proverbs 13:12. "Hope deferred makes the heart sick, but when the desire comes, it's a tree of life." I want to talk to you about this word hope. I think the hardest thing for any believer to recover from is disappointment. Disappointment comes when something I've hoped for doesn't come to pass.

That is a very hard place to recover from because hope is the seed of faith. When I operate in hope and in faith and things don't happen the way I thought they were going to happen, there is a potential for my hope being deferred, for my hope to be shattered. Then that makes me sick as a believer.

The reason it makes me sick is that I won't hope again with the same tenacity and with the same vigor. I hope just a little less. Anytime there's more disappointment and I don't deal with it properly, I hope a little less and a little less and a little less. I start praying very nominal prayers. I start praying very, very simple prayers because I don't want to believe big. I don't want to hope big. I don't want to have big faith because I'm afraid that I'm going to be disappointed. I start praying a little more generic; praying a little less faith-based. I start praying with less hope. That happens because the Bible says "hope deferred makes the heart sick."It hurts anyone, believer or not, to hope and not have it come to pass.

But the Scripture tells us that when the desire is met, it's a tree of life. When we pray for something and it comes to pass, that's a tree of life. When you pray for something, when you seek out something and the outcome isn't what you thought, there are a couple of things that you have to consider.

The first thing is that God sometimes says no for our own protection. I can't tell you how many things I've prayed for something that never happened. In the end I usually say, "God, I'm so grateful that you didn't let that happen; it would have been a mess." He closed the door, but in the moment, I was incredibly disappointed.Sometimes when things don't seem to be coming together it is because I have to war differently. The enemy is coming against what I'm praying for! There are times I need to war against the plans of the enemy!

Always remember our hope is not the outcome. Our hope is in the person of Jesus Christ. I hope in Him, and if I hope in Him, my heart will never be deferred. I'm hoping in who He is, in His goodness, in His kindness and in His faithfulness. I can get hurt, I can get sad, I can have expectations that are not met. But when my desire is truly His will, it becomes a tree of life to my soul.

It's not just my plan; it's more than my plan. That desire is not simply what I want, it's me aligning myself with what He wants.Initially my reaction might be, "God, this is not what I want." This is not what I want for me. As you walk it out, it now becomes your desire and it's exactly what you want. You just didn't know it! My hope is not planted in a person or a prayer or an outcome. My hope is planted in the character of God and , when I attach my desire to His desire, then that becomes the tree of life. With this fruit flowing in me and moving in me, I'm able to walk in joy, not disappointment.

God doesn't want us to pray timid prayers or indecisive prayers. He wants us to pray with tenacity, hope and faith because we trust that He is a good God, a faithful God and a righteous God. He is working all things together for good for those who love Him and are called according to His purpose. He has plans for us of hope and a future. If we begin to pray in that way, we're aligning ourselves with the things of God. We're aligning ourselves with the truth of who God is, and our hope becomes wrapped up in who He is.

Today, I don't know if you are feeling hopeless. I don't know if you are praying for things that haven't come to pass and you're saying, "God, I don't get it." Today begin to thank Him for His character and for who He is. I want you to begin to bless Him because He is King of Kings and Lord of Lords. I want you to exalt Him and, as you do that child of God, hope is going to arise in you. It's impossible that it doesn't. Then your desire is going to align with His desire and, when that happens, hope will rise in you and it will be like the tree of life.

Lets Pray: Lord, I lift up Your children. I pray that You encourage them and challenge them. Father, if anyone feels hope deferred, God, that You would touch them today with healing and peace and grace. I pray God that You would anoint them; You would watch over them. Father, I pray You would allow us to be people filled with hope and filled with faith, not in the outcome of things, but in who you are God. We trust that You are exactly who You say You are: our Healer, our Deliverer, our God, our King and our soon returning Messiah. Father we give You all things today, God. Father, we align our desires with Your desires, and we believe God that those things will cause a tree of life to develop within us where we'll have fruit and life and joy bubbling out of us. We thank You for all that You've done. In Jesus' Name. Amen and Amen.

The Head and Not the Tail

"The Lord will make you the head and not the tail. You shall be above only and not beneath, if you heed the commandment of the Lord your God, which I have commanded you today and are careful to observe them."
Deuteronomy 28:13 NKJV

I want to share a verse from Deuteronomy 28:13 where it says, "The Lord will make you the head and not the tail. You shall be above only and not beneath, if you heed the commandment of the Lord your God, which I have commanded you today and are careful to observe them." Now go back and read that verse out loud! I want to talk to you about this, because it is the desire of God's heart that His children be above and never beneath. This is an amazing promise! But it does have some conditions, and that is this: "If you will obey the word which I have spoken to you today, and you will observe it."

So, you want to be the head and not the tail, and always be above and never beneath? Great!

How do you get to that point? You must obey the Word of the Lord. There is a concept of Christianity where we can learn how to do all the right things, say the right things and play religious games. This is not a Christian that pleases God. A true sign of a Christian is obedience. When you recklessly obey the totality of scripture, then this promise becomes effective in your life. You become the head and not the tail. You become above always and never beneath.

You want that kind of life child of God? Then you must learn to live a life that is completely surrendered in obedience to the Word. Focus on it, put it in front of you, in your line of sight, clear, so that as you obey the word, it will lead you. You will be able to live a true Christian life of obedience and not be merely a cultural Christian, paying lip service to God.

It doesn't matter where you go to church, how much money you give, how well you speak or how beautifully you sing. If you are not obeying the word of God, you are not living the life Christ has called you to live.The mark of a child of God, is a life of obedience, and this brings the favor of God. An obedient life opens the door for favor and then you will find that you are the head and not the tail, always be above and never beneath. God will constantly be working on your behalf.

Even for a moment, if it looks like He's shifting you down to move you up, don't lose heart; He does that. But He's God. You will always come out on top, if you live a life of obedience. And so I challenge you today, child of God, obey the Lord recklessly. Obey whatever He says. Honor Him in the totality of scripture and watch Him make you the head and not the tail.

Lets Pray: God, I pray that You would lead each one reading today, that You would guide them, and make them the head and not the tail. Give them the courage to obey the totality of Your Word and, as they do that, may Your blessings and favor become part of their lives. Lord, make them the head and not the tail. Set them above and never beneath, and we give You all the praise in Jesus' name. Amen.

Nothing Should Rob Your Worship

"I will bless the Lord at all times;
His praise will continually be in my mouth."
Psalms 34:1 NKJV

In February of 2019, my best friend passed away suddenly. We were best friends since childhood; we were inseparable our whole lives. He went on to be with the Lord suddenly, with no warning. I had spoken with him only four days before he died. When I heard of his passing my heart was broken and in pain, but I walked with the peace of God. I felt His peace around me. I felt His grace. I felt His mercy. I spoke to his family when he passed and they felt the same thing. We didn't know why it happened, but we trusted the Who. We trusted God. We knew that He was a good God, and so we walked in that mercy and that understanding.

During this time, something kept playing in my spirit and in my heart. It was a verse found in Psalms 34:1. "I will bless the Lord at all times; His praise will continually be in my mouth." I will bless the Lord at all times; His praise will continually be in my mouth.It's really easy to bless the Lord and to worship and praise Him when everything is good and when I understand all things.

That, in truth child of God, is not real praise. It's not real worship. True praise, true worship, is an act of faith. When I can see that everything is good, it doesn't require any faith to worship. But when things don't look the way I think they should look or something suddenly happens that is devastating, to still be able to worship, that's where the big boys and the big girls come in. That is when maturity and true faith comes into play.

Our job as children of God is to bless the Lord at all times. It doesn't matter what you're walking through. Some of you are walking through really difficult seasons. I want you to be in the habit of worship, of worshiping the Lord at all times. Let His praise continuously flow out of your mouth. What flows out of your mouth, flows out of your heart.If praise and worship are not flowing out of your mouth, then maybe something in your heart is not flowing the way it should.

Condition yourself to have praise and worship continuously flowing out of your mouth, regardless of what you see, regardless of what you know because God is worthy. God is worthy. God is worthy at all times to be praised and to be lifted up, and so I will bless the Lord. I will bless Him. I will give Him praise. I will give Him honor. I will give Him glory because He is good, because He is faithful. He is omniscient. He is omnipresent. He is God. He is a big God and I am little me. I have no way of understanding His ways. His ways are not my ways. His ways are higher than my ways. I don't have to understand all things. I don't have to understand the why of things. I have to trust the Who of things.I have to trust who God is and who God has always been. I don't have to understand all things, but I have to bless Him because that's true, true worship. I will bless the Lord at all times. His praise will continually be in my mouth.

Whatever you're walking through, don't let anything rob your praise. Don't let anything rob your song. Don't let anything rob your continuous blessing of the Lord.Declare it all the time, in the good, the bad, the ugly, in the known, in the unknown. I will bless the Lord at all times. His praise will continually be in my mouth. Whatever you're walking through, lift up your hands and worship. Lift up your hands and praise Him.

The second I heard about my friend, and had gathered all the information, and realized this wasn't some big misunderstanding,

I went into my kitchen and played 'What a Beautiful Name' by Hillsong. And I worshiped because I knew his heart, my friend's heart, would be that his death would not rob us of our worship – that would be a horrible, horrible mistake.

I sat there and I worshiped the Lord in my grief and in my sorrow because, regardless of what was happening, He is still worthy. Nothing should rob you of lifting your hands and raising your voice before the Lord.I will. It's an act of your will and an act of your choice. I will bless the Lord at all times. His praise will continually be in my mouth. That's a habitual behavior. Continuously be in my mouth.

Lets Pray: Father, I pray that nothing would rob our song, Lord God. Nothing would rob our praise. That we would lift up our hands and worship regardless of what we are walking through because great is Your name, Jesus. We bless You today, God, and we declare Your will and Your purpose and Your strength over all things, Father. In Jesus' Name. Amen.

Faith in Action

"If you believe in your heart and do not doubt at all, you can speak to this mountain and tell it to be cast in the sea, and it shall be done."
Matthew 21:21 NKJV

Matthew 21:21 says, "If you believe in your heart and do not doubt at all, you can speak to this mountain and tell it to be cast in the sea, and it shall be done." The Lord is saying, if you have faith and don't doubt at all, you can speak to this mountain and it will be cast in the sea. Let's take a couple of minutes and study this concept, because I want us to understand what God is saying to us.

He's saying, if you have faith and faith in Him, faith in the power of God, faith in His ability, faith in who He is and don't doubt in your heart, you can speak to the mountain.Here's the connection. I can have faith; I can say I have faith. However, faith requires an action; faith requires a step. I can have all the faith in the world and keep it to myself, but that is not faith. Faith requires action; faith requires an outward demonstration of that faith.

The Lord says speak to the mountain. He doesn't say look at the mountain; He doesn't say pray to the mountain. He says speak to it. He says speak your faith out loud. Speak to the mountain and command it to be tossed into the sea and it will happen. There is an action that's happening with your faith. God is saying, "Here's your faith, that's fine. Now, speak it out. Speak it out to the mountain."

What is the mountain? All of us have a different mountain. All of our mountains are not the same. Some of our mountains are sickness; some of our mountains are bills; some of our mountains are circumstances. The Lord says, "Take your faith, believe me that I'm going to change these circumstances; believe I'm going to move them and speak it out!"

Why does God use a picture of a mountain? Because a mountain is unmovable. A mountain is massive, huge, and thick. In human hands, it is impossible to move. It is embedded in the ground; it cannot be moved. He didn't say to speak to this flower that you can just pull out with your own hand. That doesn't require great faith. He didn't even say speak to this tree. He said, "Speak to this mountain." Something that is so embedded into the bedrock of the earth. He says, "Speak to it and cast into the sea."

Each one of us has a different mountain. They are big, massive and they're embedded in front of us. We don't know how to move them on our own. The Lord is saying, "You can move them. Just take your faith and begin to declare forward. Begin to speak it out." He isn't saying, "Ask the mountain." He is saying, "Command the mountain." Take the authority He's given you as a child of God and command that mountain in front of you to move. Command it to get out of your way. Command it to not only move, but to be utterly cast into the sea; away, disintegrated, gone, in the Name of Jesus. You take your faith, verbalize it and speak out with authority.

We need to stop asking these mountains to move, or begging or pleading with them. We have authority. I have authority as a daughter of God. You have authority as a son or daughter of God to speak to the mountain in front of you and command it to move. It will be cast in the sea; it will be thrown into the sea at your command. You may say, "I've prayed. I've declared but things haven't moved." You don't stop. You keep declaring. You keep moving. You keep acting out on your faith. Faith is what moves the situations in front of us. Faith in action. Catch that: Faith in action moves the mountains in front of us.

It's faith that allows these circumstances to be disintegrated in front of us. These things that are bedrocks in front of us. Faith in action is what moves them. I don't know what mountain you're facing. I just know, child of God, you have the authority over it. You have the authority to speak to it, and command it to go, and to stand right there and not be moved until it is cast into the sea.

Lets Pray: Father, I pray today for Your children and for every mountain that stands in front of them. I pray for those who are praying for a wayward child, those who are praying for financial freedom, those who are praying for healing in their bodies, those who are praying for the restitution of their marriage, God. I speak to their mountains in the name of Jesus. I command them to be utterly tossed into the sea today, Lord God. I pray that freedom would come and the bedrocks that stand in front of them would disintegrate, God. I pray that they would be cast into the sea and completely gone, and their paths would be made straight. Put your hand upon Your children, God. Remind them of the authority they have to declare, to speak, to trust. We give You all the praise, all the honor, all the glory, in Jesus' Name. Amen.

The Same Spirit

"But if the Spirit of Him who raised Jesus from the dead dwells in you, He who raised Christ from the dead will also give life to your mortal bodies through His spirit who dwells in you."
Romans 8:11 NKJV

I pray that your heart is open to hear what God is saying to us today. We need to get into the habit of not reading the Scripture one dimensionally. I want you to begin to pray and ask God to reveal the Scripture to you, so you don't just have a knowledge, but you have an understanding of it.

With understanding, I can actually apply the Word, because now it's true to me. I have a revelation of the Word of God.

Before you read the Word, pray that God will reveal the Word to you, not just one dimensionally, but multi-dimensionally, because we serve a multidimensional God.

The verse I want to share with you today is found in Romans 8:11. It says, "But if the Spirit of Him who raised Jesus from the dead dwells in you, He who raised Christ from the dead will also give life to your mortal bodies through His spirit who dwells in you." Another way of saying that is 'the same Spirit that raised Christ from the dead now dwells in you.' He will quicken you. I want you to begin to just let that marinate in your head for a minute. The same Spirit that raised Christ from the dead, now child of God, dwells in you.

The Holy Spirit now lives in you and He will quicken your

mortal bodies. What does that mean? He will give you the ability to do anything. He is the God of the impossible. He will also give eternal life. It's not a one dimensional thing when it says He will quicken your mortal body. It's not just one level; it's multi level. It's life abundant. It's the more that He has for you. It's the ability to defeat sin. It's the ability to stand your ground. It's the ability to walk in the Truth. It's the ability to be holy. It's the ability to be empowered. It's the ability to live forever. All those things are wrapped into that one word quicken.

The same Spirit that dwells in Christ now lives in you and me and now our spirits are quickened. We're no longer turtles trying to run a race. We have now become Energizer Bunnies running a race, because that same Spirit, the Holy Spirit that raised Christ from the dead is now working in us.

If you begin to understand that and live in it, there is nothing that you cannot overcome. There is nothing that God cannot do through you. He will quicken you. He will advance you. He will advance your mortal bodies.

They thought they had Jesus beat in the grave and all their troubles were over; they had killed their troublemaker. They thought that this man that caused them so much trouble was dead. But the Holy Spirit quickened Him and He brought Him back. He brought Him back completely and totally, and it flipped the world. Flipped the world! That same Spirit that flipped the world now dwells in you and me.

Digest that for a minute.

Let that go into your heart.

Let that go into your spirit.

Oftentimes, we use this verse on Easter. However, it's not just an Easter verse. It's an everyday verse. That same Spirit that raised

Christ from the dead dwells, not visits, but dwells in us. He lives there. He quickens us on a daily basis, if we'll allow Him to.

Pray this daily. Lord, quicken my spirit, quicken my mortal body to be what You've called me to be, to walk the way You want me to walk. I thank You for eternal life, God. And Father, I thank You for everything else that comes with eternal life.

Lets Pray: Lord, I pray for those reading today that they would have a revelation that the Spirit that raised Christ from the dead is now at work in their mortal bodies. I pray that You quicken them, Lord God. You move them forward. You advance them, Lord God. You enable them and You would empower them, Lord God. There is nothing they cannot defeat. There is nothing that they cannot do, God. You quicken their life and You stretch out Your hand over them, Lord God. Touch them with Your grace and Your glory. May they not look at this verse as an Easter verse. May they look at it as a life verse. The same Spirit that raised Christ from the dead now dwells in us. We give you praise in Jesus' Name. Amen.

How Excellent is Your Name

"Oh Lord our God, how excellent is Your name in all the earth. Who have set Your glory above the heavens. Out of the mouth of babes and infants, You have ordained strength. Because of Your enemies, You have silenced the enemies and the adversaries. When I consider the heavens and the work of Your fingers, the moon and the stars which You have ordained, what is man that You are mindful of him and the son of man that You would visit him?"
Psalm 8:1 NKJV

Today's word is found in Psalm 8:1, "Oh Lord our God, how excellent is Your name in all the earth. Who have set Your glory above the heavens. Out of the mouth of babes and infants, You have ordained strength. Because of Your enemies, You have silenced the enemies and the adversaries. When I consider the heavens and the work of Your fingers, the moon and the stars which You have ordained, what is man that You are mindful of him and the son of man that You would visit him?"

Over the years, I have had the pleasure of going around the world and seeing many beautiful landscapes. One of them is Alaska, which is spectacularly beautiful. The mountain ranges, the sky and the stars. Another amazing place is Africa where the trees, animals, and all of what God has made are just so beautiful and breathtaking. The Bible says God has ordained all these things, the moon and the stars and the heavens. He's ordained them and He has stooped down even to ordain praise out of the mouth of babes. Then the Psalmist says, "You God, who are so excellent and so great and so marvelous, what is man that you are mindful of him?"

Why does He think about us, and who is the son of man that He even considers us? Why would He even choose to sit with us? God is so excellent and beautiful and we are so small in comparison. Yet, He is mindful of us and cares about us.

What I want you to embrace today is the greatness of your God. How excellent, how great, and how complete is His name? Take a moment to sit and meditate on His unfathomable greatness and excellence. Our God ordained the sun, the moon and the stars. Take in deep breaths in His presence and marvel at His goodness all around you. Say to Him, "How great is Your name, my God? How excellent are You, God? You have ordained the sun and all of the heavenly hosts, and yet you take the time to think about me. You take the time to care about me."

The Bible says that not one hair of my head falls to the ground that God doesn't know about. He has numbered them all. Not one tear falls from my eye without His awareness. He knows everything about you and he cares about everything that concerns you. There is nothing that falls outside of God's radar.

I encourage you to meditate on the greatness of your God. He is great and greatly to be praised. How excellent is His name in all the earth? It is in His name that I bless you today!

Lets Pray: Father, I pray that everyone reading today would remember that you are excellent, that you are great, and that you have ordained and created all things. Regardless of what we have been taught in science classrooms, Lord God, we are not here by mistake or chance. Your hand fashioned and designed us and your divine excellence is seen in all that you do. Father, we thank you God that your mindful of us and that you care about us. Your hand is upon us as a loving Father.

We marvel today at Your excellence and greatness ask that You would have Your way in us and through us. We bless you in Jesus name. Amen and amen.

Does Your Heart Look Like Jesus?

"Search me, oh God and know my heart. Try me and know my anxieties. See if there be any wicked way of me and lead me in the way everlasting."
Psalm 139:23 NIV

What does your heart look like? Psalm 139:23 provides us with a picture of what our hearts should look like. It says, "Search me, oh God and know my heart. Try me and know my anxieties. See if there be any wicked way of me and lead me in the way everlasting." I think we would all love to think that we are completely sanctified, perfect, and that our intentions are always right and good. Although, the Psalmist makes it very clear that our intentions are not always the best.

David knew this and shows us that he could not rely on his own goodness by choosing to relinquish control of his own heart to God. He does not say, "God, I'll search myself, and I'll let you know." He's said, "God, you search me. God, you try me. You search my heart, God. You expose my anxieties. You expose the wickedness that's in me."

The truth is, though we do not want to think about it, there is wickedness in each of us. We are still flesh. That old nature might be crucified daily, but it still tries to live every day. Ungodliness, bad expectations, and a multitude of other things that displease God are alive and well in us. That is the truth. Anything less than that is a lie. We do have wickedness within us, but the Psalmist says, "Here Lord, expose the wickedness in me and lead me in the way everlasting."

It is not good enough just to know that there's wickedness. We cannot simply say, "Hey, I have an issue with this." We have to turn and begin to walk in a way that's godly. It's not enough for me to just acknowledge what is wrong with me. I have to acknowledge and then proceed to walk in righteousness and turn away from the wicked way.

As a child of God, you need to understand today that part of your responsibility as a maturing follower of Jesus is to allow the Holy Spirit to search you. This is the deal, when God begins to expose what is in your heart, you do not have the right to fight Him. You don't get to say, "But God, this…" or "But God, that…" No. When he exposes it, you repent, and you turn.

You ask the same Holy Spirit to give you the strength to overcome. We cannot search our own hearts because we are biased. We will either be hard on ourselves, or too easy. Let the Holy Spirit do the work. Our job is to have our ears open so we can hear Him. God will put you in situations to expose your anxiety and to expose the things that don't please Him. When he exposes wickedness, then you can ask Him to lead you in the way that is everlasting.

Your conversation with the Lord may go something like this, "God, how do I walk with You, now that You have shown me that I have a problem with fits of rage, issues with envy, jealousy, and hatred? All these things are in my heart, now God, lead me in the way that is everlasting. Lead me in the way that pleases you."

Listen, Child of God, you were not put on earth just to be a good Christian. You were put here to become like Jesus. Everything about you is subject to the Word of God. There is nothing about you that cannot be touched by the Lord unless you prevent it. If you say "No, God, I'm good just like this. You are not allowed to touch that, God." On the other hand, if you are truly honest, saying, "God, I want to walk after you," then there is nothing He can't touch and make new.

There's nothing he can't point his finger to and say, "That right there, I want that, because that doesn't bring me glory and that doesn't look like me. I want everything about you to look like me."

So I'm going to challenge you today. How much do you look like Jesus? Are there things in you that don't look like Jesus?

Let's get them in line. Let's begin to walk in the way that's righteous. Let's begin to walk in the way that's everlasting. Let's begin to get rid of the things in us that don't look like Jesus. Every day, allow the Holy Spirit to search you and move you in a way that's everlasting because it's time to reflect Him in all that we do, all that we say, and all that we are. We can all talk a good game. We can even look a certain way, right? But God is saying in this verse, "Let's deal with the heart. Let's make the heart reflect Jesus, not just the façade."

Lets Pray: Father, I pray, Lord God, for all those reading. I pray, God. that you encourage every heart and that you would allow each person to know that you are with them, God, and that you are doing a sacrificial work in them. You are doing a consecrating work in their heart, God. It is your deep desire to shape us and fashion us into the image of Jesus. Father, today, the question that you're asking us is "does your heart look like Jesus?" Father, we just lay before you and we ask your Holy Spirit to search us, to know us, to try us, to expose that which is wicked and then to lead us in the way that's everlasting.

Father, I pray that you search us today. You search each one of us, Lord God, and that you would allow us to obediently walk after you until all our ways reflect you, Jesus. In Jesus name, Amen!

Get On the Right Train

"Casting down every argument and every high thing that exalts itself against the knowledge of God, taking in captivity every thought into the obedience of Christ Jesus."
2 Corinthians 10:5 NKJV

There is a battle going on inside of your mind! In 2 Corinthians 10:5 the Bible says, "casting down every argument and every high thing that exalts itself against the knowledge of God, taking in captivity every thought into the obedience of Christ Jesus." This verse gives us a blueprint for our battles. I want you to think for a minute about your thoughts and how many things we think about in the course of a day. I want you to imagine for a minute that your thoughts are like a train and whatever thought you start with, takes you on a ride. So you get up in the morning to travel to work. You grab your coffee and you run out and, without even realizing it, you hopped on the wrong train. You get on the wrong train because you're not paying attention and, now, you're stuck on that train for a little bit before you can actually turn around and go back– your thoughts are the same way.

They start you on a journey. When you wake up in the morning, whatever thoughts you give room to, whatever place you give room to, they're going to take you on a journey. They're going to take you on a destination. That's why the Lord is clear. He says, "Take every thought into captivity." That means lock it up.

Thoughts that are not of Jesus, thoughts that are not godly, thoughts that are sinful, thoughts that are not edifying, thoughts that don't benefit you– take them captive. Take them, lock them up. Don't get on the metaphorical train of bad thoughts. Lock them up in obedience to Christ Jesus. Why? Because you want your mind to be the mind of Christ.

So if you allow thoughts of fear, anxiety, depression, discouragement, sin, sexual sin, sexual thoughts, impure thoughts, murderous thoughts, anger, or hostility into your mind, they are going to take you on a journey. There is a chance that you can get stuck on this train for the whole day, if you choose to never get off. You want to make sure that whatever you're meditating on, whatever you're thinking about, whatever is going through your head, is of Christ. If it's not, the scripture says, take it hostage.

Cast it out and lock it up. Don't allow it. The second those thoughts come up, recognize it's not from Jesus. Your thoughts need to be. "I don't want any part of it. I'm not going on that train. I'm going on a different train" and get on the right train for your day. Get on the right train for what God wants you to have because if you get on the wrong train, you'll find yourself not believing, not growing your faith, and not stretching. If you get on the right train, you've set yourself up to succeed and you've set your day up to succeed.

You start thinking God's thoughts. You start thinking of things that are of Jesus. You start thinking what the scriptures say, things that are good and wholesome and righteous and godly. You allow your mind to start there and you take those other thoughts captive, you won't find yourself in the wrong place.

So child of God, what thoughts are you giving room to? What are you allowing to germinate in your brain?

I'll tell you what. Whatever you're thinking about, it's going to begin to seep into your heart. Whatever you're dreaming about, whatever you are allowing in your thoughts or even absently thinking about, that will harm you. Be very careful about what you are thinking about. All of our battles happen in our thoughts right here.

Can I tell you something? Most things that you're going to think and worry about are going to be bigger than you, but they're not bigger than Him. Whatever your struggle, whatever you're walking with, set your thoughts straight. That is where you begin. You get your mind right and, as a result, you're going to get your life right. You get your mind right and, as a result, you're going to get your heart right. You're going to get your mind right and, as a result, you're going to get everything else to fall in line.

Begin to fix these thoughts. Make them godly. Scripture says, take them captive. Every single thought that's not from Jesus, take it captive to obedience to His word. The sin coming up in your mind, push it down. Don't allow it to have a place but instead allow His thoughts to fill your heart and your mind. You will see a different day and you'll walk into a different outcome. Get on the right train.

Lets Pray: Father, I pray for your people, that they would learn what it is to take their thoughts captive, Lord God. To get on the train that you've picked for them, the road that you've picked for them, Lord God. That their hearts and their minds will be filled with thoughts of you and your word and your truth, Lord God. That your freedom would dwell in their minds and in their hearts and any thoughts that they struggle with God, that you give them the courage to take it captive and push it away and fill it with what is true and what is of you. We give you this week, we give you this day. We thank you, God, that we have the grace for whatever's coming this day and that you have already declared us victorious. We give you praise in Jesus' name. Amen.

Lord Revive Us

"Lord, I've heard of your fame of old.
I stand in awe of your deeds, Lord. Renew them in our day."
Habakkuk 3:2 NIV

This is our 60th devotional! What a journey we have taken together. It has been my honor to walk with you through this book! For our last devotional, I want to convey to you what I believe God is saying in this time and in this season. Habakkuk 3:2 says, "Lord, I've heard of your fame of old. I stand in awe of your deeds, Lord. Renew them in our day." Let me tell you we are in a season, in a time in history, when God wants to renew His work, to renew His glory in the midst of His Church. Can I tell you that, as a people, we have yet to see the power of God unfold? We have yet to see God move in our midst.

The reason is that the Church has forgotten how to be the Church. The Church has allowed a lot of junk into it. We have forgotten what it is to be holy. We have forgotten what it is to live righteously. We have forgotten what it is to pray. We have forgotten what it is to believe for the supernatural. Because of that, we've allowed a lot of junk into the Church. We've ceased to be the watchmen that we're supposed to be. We've compromised with the world. We've allowed the culture of the world into the Church. We keep using the term "culture of the world," but it's really not "culture." The Scripture calls it principalities and rules. We've allowed dark things to come into the Church and we've forgotten how to be the Church.

Instead of standing on our own two feet as the Church, we've cowered and we've bent down to the things of the world. What has happened is that the power has left the Church and now we are not seeing people healed. We are not seeing people delivered. We are not seeing people set free. And yet, that is the heart of God. He said He came to set the captives free. He came to heal the broken hearted. He came to set at liberty those that are bound up - that is the heart of God, and yet we're not seeing it because the power has left the Church.

God, today, in this season and in this time, wants to renew His power. He wants to renew His faith. What Habakkuk was saying is, "Lord, I know what You did in the past. I've heard the stories. I've heard about the people that You've healed and the things that You've done. I don't want to hear about it, God. I want You to do it in my time. I want to see it with my own eyes." I pray that as I'm speaking to You, that becomes the prayer of Your heart.

"God, I know what You did in the Book of Acts. I know what You did in the Gospels. I want You to renew it today. I want You to see it with my own eyes. I want to see it, God. I want to participate in the supernatural. I want to see the cancer rot in front of my eyes. I want to see people set free. I want to see the dead raised. I want to see miracles. I want to see liberty. I want to see people who walk into church bound, walk out free. I want to see You move, God. I want to see You big, bold and on display." I cannot see the Church be anything less anymore. Earlier in this book there was a devotional entitled "No More Grasshoppers." And that's the truth. The Church has chosen to be grasshoppers when they're supposed to be lions.

This beats in my personal heart so strongly because God has called me and appointed me to be an igniter, an equipper, and an awakener to the Body. God called me into full time itinerant preaching to be a tool to revive the Church. That is my call, being a revivalist to the Church and allowing God to use me to awaken the Church.

In the summer of 2019, I took a ridiculously radical step of obedience. At the leading of the Lord, I resigned from the church I served in for 15 years. I resigned because I believed that the calling on my life right now is to see the Church come alive. So I'm committed to this verse. I'm committed to see God on display, big, bold and powerful, watching the Church become the Church.

I'm excited for this season. I pray that you would begin to desire revival in your own heart, in your church, in your spheres of influence. I pray that you would not allow any more deadness in you, deadness in your house, deadness in your church. No more deadness. It's time for God's work to be renewed in our day, in our time.

So I encourage you to step out and begin to seek revival. Revival doesn't come because we're full. Revival comes because we're desperate. Revival comes because we want God to move. We want God to show up. That's when revival shows up.

So, today, if you want God to move in your life, just begin to call out to Him. Say, "God, I want You to revive my heart, revive my home, revive my church!"

When I stepped out in obedience, I didn't have a Plan B. There was no job waiting for me. I'm stepped out completely on the water, believing that God had called me, believing that He was going to show up and make a way for me if I just honored His voice. I believe that I'm right in the pocket of what God wants this time and this season. And I believe God is going to use me for His glory. IT IS TIME FOR REVIVAL!

Lets Pray: Father, we give You praise and we thank You, Lord God, for all the things that You've done in the past. Lord God, we thank You for Your works of old. God, we thank You for the miracles that we can look to in history and in Scripture and say,

"Look what God has done."

But Father, we're not satisfied with reading the Book of Acts. We want to live the Book of Acts, God. And so I pray, God, that You would bring revival to every one of our hearts, to every home, to every leader, Lord God. Father, I pray that You would bring revival to the Church.

Lord, help us to make Your name famous in this earth, Lord God. And Lord, may the Church of America, never be the same again, Lord God. We cry out for revival, God, in our personal life, in our nation, in our churches. Revive us, we pray in Jesus' Name. Amen.

About the Author

Pastor Marsha Mansour emigrated to the United States from Egypt with her family at the age of three. She is a graduate of Zion Bible Institute, Providence, RI and was the first Egyptian female ordained minister of the Assemblies of God on the East Coast. She is a conference and convention speaker who was on the pastoral staff at Evangel Church, Scotch Plains, N.J, for 15 years, and has served in a pastoral capacity for more than two decades. In 2015, God led Pastor Marsha to release her first book, "The Courage To Live" filled with personal testimonies of God's power and faithfulness! In 2019, Pastor Marsha released her second book, "The Courage to Lead" that truly speaks to the heart of every leader. On September 8, 2019, Pastor Marsha resigned from her Family Life Pastor position at Evangel Church, following the call of God to be a fulltime Revivalist! Her passion is to see the church walk in God's Fullness!